RECOVERING THE GROUND

RECOVERING THE GROUND

Critical Exercises in Recollection

William H. Poteat

State University of New York Press

Front cover:
NIKE by E. Moustakas

Published by
State University of New York Press, Albany

Printed in the United States of America

For information, address State University of New York Press,
State University Plaza, Albany, N.Y. 12246

Production by M. R. Mulholland
Marketing by Bernadette La Manna

Library of Congress Cataloging-in-Publication Data

Poteat, William H.
Recovering the ground : critical exercises in recollection / William H. Poteat.
p. cm.
Includes bibliographical references and index.
ISBN 0-7914-2131-7 (alk. paper). — ISBN 0-7914-2132-5 (pbk. : alk. paper)
1. Philosophy, American—20th century. I. Title.
B945.P69R43 1994
191—dc20 93-45489
CIP

10 9 8 7 6 5 4 3 2 1

For Patricia . . .

Lay your sleeping head, my love,
Human on my faithless arm.

W. H. Auden

Today's nihilism is no *Angst* and all play. . . .
The dizzying horror of the abyss is replaced by the virtuosity of performance—
a kind of perpetual mid-air tap dance, in which the ground isn't needed. . . .

—Susan Shell

Knowing where you stand is knowing who you are.

—Eudora Welty

We can learn at last to say: 'All knowledge comes to this, that existence is enough. . . .'

—W. H. Auden

How is that faith achieved (the supposed faith that the things of our world exist), how expressed, how deepened, how threatened, how lost? . . . I do not propose the idea of acknowledging as an alternative to knowing but rather as an interpretation of it. . . .

—Stanley Cavell

Acknowledgments

It is a pleasure to thank the estimable women of the Department of Religion support staff at Duke University who, on top of their regular chores, superintended the transfer of my thoughts to floppy disks with just the right mix of professional aplomb and sassiness: Debbie Gray, Becky Hayes, Christie Tyson, and Darleen Hatherly.

Thanks, too, to the one who makes it all go: Wanda Camp.

Note: Material on pp. 161–185 has, in slightly different form, appeared in *Listening: A Journal of Religion and Culture* (Winter, 1994)

Prolegomenon

Some seven and a half miles west southwest of where I write a seaman, bidding us to call him Ishmael, signed aboard the Pequod to rid himself of "a damp, drizzly November of the soul" and ended, alive, clinging to a coffin in the sea.

I gaze Northeastward across the Atlantic and think of her fierce winter rages blowing down from the Pole. I linger over these two emblems, Ahab's monomaniac rebelliousness against a mysterious, malign, and intractable order of things and nature's watery power declaring itself against man's puny boasts—and I wonder: can we survive our mellenial addiction to gnostic apocalypticism; can we once again affirm the good creation, our mortal home; can we yet recover our ground?

Gnosticism, older than the Western world, an everpresent religion deep in the Western soul, forever at once concealing itself and challenging its proscription by Christianity as a heresy, is the belief that men and women are pure spirits, now held captive in the prison of this world created by an evil demiurge from which alone esoteric gnosis can set them free. Possessed of this salvific knowledge, mankind, now in its own power knowing who it is and where home is, sets about to cast off its bondage to a world conceived and brought forth in malice in order to give reign to pure, untrammeled spirits and the "world"—whatever this is now to be—that such as these would fashion.

For ancient gnosticism this was to be achieved by

various forms of *askesis*—strenuous disciplines either to release spirit from its entanglement within our material, sensuous prisonhouse or to mortify the power of matter by an exhausting life of sensuality. In either case, it was a matter for each man or woman to attend to for himself or herself as a culture of the spirit.

Only with Joachim of Fiori (twelfth Century) did gnosticism acquire a philosophy of history with implications for action projected into an age to come, portending a heavenly kingdom on earth ruled by spirit, no longer subject to earthly conditions of whose lineaments the initiated had present knowledge. The incoherency of such an expectation, far from inhibiting its appeal, on the contrary, made it the perfect material of gnostic dreams. It is here that our addiction truly began. The impulse to destroy everything that is given and fashion a new heaven and a new earth is the impulse of pure spirit subject only to its own self-assertion, culminating in Dostoyevski's Kirilov who declares himself to be God and suicide the earnest of his Godhood. Its influence is now so ubiquitous, so commonplace, not to say, domesticated, that a feat of extraordinary perspicacity is required to see that it pervades the institutions of this culture and is rampant in the academy. In the academy it is the rage that gives it away.

I assume that each one of us de facto affirms the intractable reality and goodness of the world in the mere fact of continuing to exist from one moment to the next and the next and the next.

I do not underestimate the force of our de jure demurrals implicated in the fact that we conceive ourselves as discarnate spirits with nothingness under foot—thanks to the combined power over our imaginations of literacy hypertrophied and of gnostic apocalypticism—to sustain our denials of this affirmation. And if you should argue that it may be only weariness that stays the hand of suicide, I shall reply that in that very weariness, even here, conservation is at work, the power of existence exerts itself, however equivocally.

It is hard to imagine how one might mitigate the alienation wrought in this culture by hypertrophied literacy and loosen the political and historical power over our institutions of gnostic dreams. Even the defeat in its own manifest irrelevancy to the interpretation of human existence and as a guide to the management of its affairs of that most cruel and unforgiving of all forms of gnostic apocalypticism, namely, militant Marxism, can afford us only the most equivocal hope at this level of existence.

If however the views have merit that I have set forth in *Polanyian Meditations* and *A Philosophical Daybook,* and advance still further in what follows, then each one of us—and as many of us as choose to come together on it—is rooted in an archaic and infrangible ground that is closer to us than we are to ourselves and that the hypertrophication of the values of literacy and discarnate spiritualism can obscure but cannot efface: Our sentient, motile and oriented mindbodies in the world that are the ground of all meaning and meaning discernment, whence all reflection derives—even the literature of gnostic dreams.

It is a scandal that the most commonplace of all facts—that we are inextricably rooted in our bodies in the world, and that we begin and end with this—should require such dialectical prodigies to establish. Yet so it is. In this book then I am making yet another payment on my project to recover the ground.

For 2500 years, more or less, first written documents and than printed books whose words were viewed as "objects" that, in being taken in by the reader's eyes, were brought to bear upon a world "out there" (as printed words themselves were "out there" to the beholding eye) made it natural to ask: What is this book *about,* upon what "objects" does it bear? It could always be said to be *about* this or that aspect of the world "out there."

In *this* sense of *about,* the present essay is not *about* anything. In its style—awkward syntax, nonlinear progression, reflexivity, dialectical reduplication, an unfamiliar and often deliberately "atonal" diction congested with what will appear to be pretentious or merely clever coinages that, together, allow my radical insight lucidly to oppose itself to the conceptual landscape from which it has been elicited and to impede yet another bemused lapse into our familiar dualisms—I have obeyed the demand upon me of this primitive reality to educe and then body forth the logos that endows my mindbody with sentience, motility, and orientation, both before I have yet spoken and after I do, as itself the condition of speech. By these same tactics I have undertaken to reach out of the pages of this "book" to drag the reader mindbodily into it in order that through the torque and sinew of its language she may be brought, even against her will—as it surely will be—to dwell in herself as her own unique place.

The reader of my text is in a relation to it quite exactly like that of a beholder of Cézanne's paintings of pine trees and rocks—he cannot work his way through to the far side of things with an unimpeded gaze because of all the boulders right in front of him that he has first to climb over. Thus he will have brought home to him and even be profoundly impressed by his own and the world's ambiguous substantiality. The reader of a good, lucid, Cartesian text, on the other hand, is like the spectator of, let us say, Ghirlandaio's "The Last Supper," who, in an instantaneous glance, can move from foreground through the picture plane to an abstract infinity.

Indeed, I think it not outrageous to say that, at many points, my text is like a fully developed Cubist painting. Cézanne began his assault upon Renaissance linear perspective by painting still lifes that simply didn't "look right": A vase and a plate seemed not to occupy "the same space"; the two halves of a single plate did not even seem to. The space inside the frame became ambiguous, polycentric, resisting closure; the beholder's position in relation to that space became equivocal; indeed one's position in the museum before the painting, even therefore his place in the world itself became problematic. In the fully developed Cubism of Picasso and Braque, the multifarious represented surfaces, contours, and protrusions of things, which hitherto had been "rationally" projected onto the canvas as an independently existing, static, three-dimensional world around which the stabile eye could "close," are now flattened out upon the canvas surface. As our being moves about upon this surface, any moment may yield a fluent organizing gestalt for some of the now "disintegrated" parts of things; therefore there is no (perspectival) center from which the eye can achieve a (perspectivally) visual closure on the whole. Instead, the center now becomes the tonic, ductile mindbody of the viewer himself.

Thus, I aspire to place the reader in an agonistic relation to the text. The rhetoric seeks by reduplication to embody dynamically in its own tension the actual intentional structure of our feats of knowing; so that we are made aware *in the reading* of how, as we pretend our focus *distally,* the *proximal ground* of this pretension is retrotended. Hence, the at times relentless reflexivity of the text. Obliquely this is a book about a radically new kind of book that is an instance of itself.

From the ground thus recovered my reflection circles and doubles back, as I have written my daily installments, frequently revisiting an earlier perplexity now come upon from a novel direction, therefore freshly seen.

How, defined by these premises, do *reflection, criticism, world, imagination, value, interpretation, thinking, speaking, time, hope, memory* begin to look?

Around the armature of this point of view my daily investigations have deliberately proceeded in a nonlinear style, like that of conversation or of thought still seeking consummation.

It would be disingenuous of me to claim that I wrote the whole of this book with a Cross porous point pen because I fully appreciated how my doing so would remove impediments to my discovering what I wished to say. But I did and *it* did. What could this possibly mean? I need to say, since, so far as this is possible—and it may well not be—the style of reading the book will have to be as unfamiliar as was the writing of it. We are working against long-standing and powerful resistance—the psychoanalytic analogy is apposite here—to recover the ground that antidates alphabetic literacy and yet is still intact, even if obscured, within our literate midst.

My mindbody's pretension toward meaning and its articulation is always wholly implicated in the activities that we discriminate as thinking, speaking, writing—whatever the instrument for this last I may be using. It is the logos that informs the whole of my mindbodily coherence that comes to be manifest in each of these according to its specific modality.

As I *write,* this logos comes to a focus, achieves articulation, and appears in the world at the precise juncture at which the nib (extra fine) of my Cross porous point pen meets the page on which I write. This extra fine point entreats me to seek for subtleties that I would otherwise ignore. A delicate instrument for thinking encourages the emergence of delicate thought.

The way in which I will apprehend my mindbody in the world in the concentering of its engagement with the world will be a function of the possibilities that are afforded in that meeting, for *at that moment* this meeting *is* my mindbodily being. If my instrument inhibits me in *writing* my thoughts, then it inhibits me in my thinking them; for writing and thinking here come to exactly the same thing.

For me to write what I have just written I had to achieve a certain unfamiliar relationship to myself, my writing, my thinking. Your reaction to my words are likely to be exactly like my own, when I abandon my role as thinker-writer and have turned back to my words and established for myself the detached relationship of a reader: How utterly preposterous! What could this possibly mean? And in any case, so what?

If I were writing instead with a broad, felt-tipped Magic Marker, not only would what I am able to feel *inclined* to write be more cryptic, less fluent—cramped—because of the awkwardness of the instrument I use; my thinking, connate as it is with the speaking-writing–and all the activities to which my mindbody is given—will therefore also be cramped, coarse, less cursive. The style, focus, and reach of my thinking is defined by the possibilities that exist for my mindbody *at this moment,* focused in the juncture of pen point and paper. *At this moment* the limits of the world are configured by my hand, my pen, and my paper. *At this moment* what is thinkable, what is imaginable are bound by these. Different instruments invite my mindbody to appear in the world as articulate thought in different ways. Different instruments induce in me different apprehensions of myself in the world; different apprehensions of the world. Unmediated viva voce speech is quite another case, of course, but susceptible of the same kind of analysis.

Had my imagination not been formed by my lifelong practice of composing the thought to which I wished to give some permanence by writing it out in my own fair hand, but had instead suffered it to be subject to the demands of the typewriter—even more so, of the word processor—my sense of the nature and provenance of my thought and the given world to which it was directed and upon which it bore once consummated would have been very different. It is hardly too much to say that otherwise I would not have conceived of the phenomenological project that has for so long engaged my attention.

Handwriting is inherently framed by the visual spatiality of the surface upon which the written words are inscribed, and by the movement through space—both visual and motor—of the writing hand and its instrument. This of course goes without saying.

My relation to the words, my relation to their meaning—written out by hand and pen, entrammeled in the living motility of my mindbody in the act of writing—are very different from my typed out words (no less, of course, subject to my hands' motor dexterity). The intervention of a mechanical device between me and my words on the typed page, imposing its own abstract and uniform pattern upon the otherwise organic flow of my thought into articulation—whatever the gains will be, and they are, of course, many—estranges my words from my lively mindbody in the world of time of which these words are the issue. The idiosyncrasies that constitute "Poteat's handwriting" have been flattened out. My typescript may have style; it cannot have a "handwriting."

The oral imagination has historical depth that the printed word and the instruments that produce it have desiccated. The oral imagination is formed by *listening,* and when it writes it writes as if it spoke, drawing my mindbody to a focus in my concrete reality as a speaker-hearer. The literate imagination, because it is alienated by print from the concrete density of my mindbody—our mindbodily life—within the rich laminations of time, moves me—leads us—toward an abstract picture of myself in the world. The literate imagination is formed by *looking,* and when it writes it writes in such a way as to draw my mindbody to a focus in the finite printed page, in which all particulars are cotemporaneously present in an instant that is a kind of "eternity". The imagination formed by a print culture is thus inclined toward shallowness: The printed words on the page cast no shadows.

Thinking that is apprehended as retaining a connection to its lively, temporal roots in my mindbody *as I write* in the time that writing *takes* (typing, of course, also takes time), that is preserved in the concrete fluency of my idiosyncratic hand, will be thinking that exhibits its historical depth, embedded in my concrete history.

There is an irony here that must not be overlooked. If I were to try to present my argument to you viva voce, profiting from all the "extralinguistic" accompaniments of our lively verbal give and take that would be afforded in our mindbodily presence to one another, I should fail. Subject as we would be to the relentless surge of the time of our oral-aural exchange, we should not have *time.* If my words are to induce the transformation to which I aspire for you and for myself, there will have to be time; time for the rhetoric of this new perspective to be incorporated, taken in, working upon those levels of your mindbodily being that, though they possess a pertinacious substantiality, are, even so, usually in the shadow that is cast by the concrete focus of your awareness at a given moment. A written or printed text alone can give us this time.

All of this is, of course, utterly exoteric. We dwell inextricably in these most intimate of all realities. Why make so much of them? Because they are realities that must be made explicit for epistemology and philosophical anthropology. If they slip into oblivion, then we shall, humanly speaking, follow them there.

In my effort then to recover for myself and for you this potent and ubiquitous, but now elusive, being in ourselves at the point of our most archaic covenant with the world—that compact alone that saves our souls from nihilism—I have had to enter my study each working day and begin a disciplined withdrawal from the levels of my imagination that are in thrall to the images and values of the printed word and discarnate, world-transcending spirit into the regions of my being that possess a pertinacious substantiality that, even so, are usually in the shadow. How am I to keep in touch with my own actual dynamic mindbody in the world of time that I shall try to deliver to myself and to you in a medium that, by the time you read these printed words, will be all but wholly abstracted from this world of actual time? By the iteration in my handwritten version—in due course to become printed text—of allusions to the ubiquitous presence of an historically situated person behind the hand that writes the sometimes agonizing unfolding of thought actually taking place in time, rather than having fallen from heaven onto the permanent page of print, the elements of which all "exist" cotemporaneously in an instant without temporal thickness.

Just to frame the whole in real time by giving a date for each day's installment is a beginning. When, at the top of this page, I write 10/15/90 the point of my pen stakes a claim to a moment in time for my existence. The abstract organizing principle of the finite visible page, all its parts cotemporaneously present in visual space, ordered by the wholly abstract device of pagination—that is, by counting!—is subordinated to the temporality of the writing process. The date places the writer *as an existent mindbody at some particular time;* it places the reader—despite the inducements in our literate culture to overlook this—in a similar relation to his or her own existence in time. When you read 10/15/90, even if it is for you 10/15/94, you locate your own existence in a moment.

Perhaps it is now possible to imagine how best to approach the reading of what follows. It would all be much easier, if it had an epistolary form, a personal letter to you in my own hand.

If however you remember as you read the *printed* page how it is that the words got there, what is being said will seem more natural, even at times commonplace: to the printer from a floppy disk, to the disk from a notebook in my own hand, to the pages of the notebook as the logos of my mindbody was drawn to a focus at the point where my Cross porous point pen flowed along the page as my thought made its verbal appearance in the world.

And if this should happen for you, as it does from time to time for me, the ground that we have surrendered, even though we have never ceased to stand upon it, will be recovered; and with it our sanity.

Nantucket Island
October 1990

Critical Exercises in Recollection

5/28/90

There is always a penumbra that envelops every act and object of our knowing and doing. This constraint, that marks the mortality of our engagement with the world, is so ingenuous that it requires the unreflected genius of a Cézanne, or else extraordinary feats of reflexive attention from the rest of us, to disclose this underived environ of our appearance in the world.

The dominant epistemological paradigm of our philosophic tradition fashions a reduction of the lively reality of our actual seeing to an abstraction wherein there can be clarity and distinctness for an inert eye gazing upon an immobile object in the stasis of a time that is an "eternity."

This abstraction immures us within a second-order account of our noetic relation to the world that persuades us that we can disembrangle ourselves from the world's and our own viscid actuality.

What we know or do never stands lucently before us because all these transactions are haunted by the presence of our mindbodies as the systematically elusive provenance and ambient ground of *all* meaning and meaning discernment.

When you behold the developed photograph you took of the Grand Canyon's vastness, both you and it were enveloped within the penumbra cast by the elusive presence of your mindbody as ambient ground. The camera lens, at once begotten by and the begetter of this culture, is but a discarnate eye. Therefore objects stand lucently before it. About the worlds that continually appear in our incessant coition with an indeterminate other the camera can only lie.

Cézanne, who said, "I wait until the landscape thinks itself in me," succeeded in some of his landscapes—including some that were entitled, "Portrait of Madame Cézanne"—in "painting" the penumbra.

Because printed words are inert, compared to those we speak and hear spoken; because if we are to read them at all, they will have to be fixed over against us in visual space within a relatively shallow focal plane; because in this static articulation (even our *motor* space is made subject to the stasis of viewing fixed objects in visual space) of the space between our eyes and the printed words our orientation to them is more efficient when it is linearly teleological, moving in a straight line toward the page; and because the ubiquitous de facto dialectical exchanges between our lively mindbodies and the world—which are often *vividly* sensed in the oral-aural reciprocity—is all but wholly obscured in our literate transactions: because of all this, the basal pretensive-retrotensive structure of our being is subordinated by this introjection of the values of literacy that are implicated with this framing of the world.

We do not begin to appreciate the extent of this forming of our sensorium, hence of our perception's, by the inheritance of literacy. For example, as a teacher, imbued with literacy values, I could not help feeling that even a handwritten term paper was not as clear—ah! yes—nor as cogent as that same paper typewritten.

The demand for coherence within the logos that at a given moment informs our living mindbody is so importunate that the paradigm of a good written-out argument surreptitiously takes on the values of a page of print—so subtle as to be discoverable only by an extraordinary feat of attention: uniform rows of words, evenly ordered lines, separated by uniform spaces, moving paragraph by paragraph along a straight line toward an architectonic telos constrained by the black rectangular mass of print that recapitulates the rectangular shape of the page upon which it appears.

In the oral-aural reciprocity, by contrast, amidst the lively give and take of colloquy, we often do not speak in complete, nor even in strictly grammatical, sentences. There is almost never even the shadow of a paragraph.

The exchange of the constraints of print and their distinctive pressure upon our mindbodily imagining and thinking for the ampler constraints of lively civil discourse—for the openness, that is, the sense of contingency of the form of its evolving—is precisely what gives freedom and liveliness to oral discourse that is elicited from within the existential reality and depth of the persons who participate. Our colloquy meanders; conclusions, when they come, are seldom explicitly remarked. But most of all our oral colloquy is tolerant of, even takes delight in, novel, even eccentric usage and in idiosyncratic speech patterns. One meets one's actual worldly fellows in this way. The tokens that bear our viva voce argument do not appear in visual space but are informed from within, like a musical phrase from Bach, through the logos that lively binds asseverations and their rejoinders into the flow of colloquy.

None of these characteristics of the oral-aural setting are viewed as flaws except from the standpoint of printed discourse. That guardian of literate rectitude, the copy editor, makes the diction, grammar and syntax of the written-out argument uniform in order that a printed text may come forth that will have good standing *sub specie aeterni,* as this would be conceived by the culture of the book.

The texts of my books are, on the contrary, designed to defeat their appropriation in order that, paradoxically, the reader will be forced to dwell in, reappropriate and come to value the logos of his or her own quotidian mindbodily life.

5/30/90

The prereflective ground of all meaning, meaning discernment, coherence, and value protends itself within our convivial mindbodily life, issues in language, and is manifest in our every authentic act of speech. The constant pretensive-retrotensive relation to this ground of our acts of speech, the most concrete of all realities, reveals this ground itself to be concrete; elusive because it is closer to us than we are to ourselves.

Romanticism, reacting, first to the rationalism of the Enlightenment and then to the growing authority and putatively antihumanistic import of science and technology sought against the prose of science and even ordinary language, to devise a special form of discourse in which to embody and thereby recover the reality of imagination, mind—beyond mere technical reason—spirit, value, and unity.

The disanalogies between the language of Newton's *Principia* and the poetry of Blake were patent and were taken in themselves to be a vindication of a special discourse for the expression of human value in a world of putatively "value-free facts." These modes of discourse could never be mistaken for one another; and in a sense that was taken to be that.

This uneasy truce had the effect of aborting a more radical inquiry that would have begun by asking: What are the *analogies* between the language of poetry and the language of science? What indeed are the analogies among *all* forms of discourse, ranging from the elliptical forms of our oral-aural reciprocity at one end to the universal languages of pure mathematics at the other—with everything in between included?

5/31/90

The dualism, in the making since the invention of alphabetic literacy, whereby the ontologically privileged written and therefore "eternal" word became the paradigm of logos as such and therefore of meaning and reality, was given its definitive modern articulation by Descartes. The ascendency of the language of mathematics in which the book of (eternal) nature was taken to be written, opposed to the evanescence of the realm of secondary qualities, served further to endorse the view that the *real* is *eternal,* that even human being is best understood when reduced to mensurable quanta of matter in motion, for it is here that it most fully participates in the eternal world of number and that therefore the language of narrative and myth, for example—language within which our quotidian, oral-aural life is lived—is problematic. It is not that we abandon these modes of discourse; we cannot. It is just that, as the prestige of science and technology becomes more omnipresently authoritative, our inescapable resort to this ordinary language of human life in time becomes the occasion of increasing self-consciousness. This deepening dissocation, while it did not bring an end to poetry and poetizing—the official theory, powerful as it was, could not weaken the human demand for the embodiment of genuine realities, *in no sense* lacking ontological authority, that only poetry could achieve—*did* defer, even to the present, the asking of the radical question concerning the *analogies*—whatever their patent disanalogies—between the language of number and that of poesy.

The fact that reflection upon these matters was carried out in the "theater of solitude"[a] ensured that the attention could not be drawn to a reality that underlay the dualism that gave rise in the first place to the obsession with the priority of science over poetry.

All forms of our discourse—and I do not for present purposes exclude the language (and its syntax) of gesture, including the gross disposition of the body in its postures—however various are their many formal properties and however rich or poor their "semantic" resources, equally derive from and remain dependent upon the logos that is implicated in the primitive ordinations of our mindbodies, derive their authority as vectors of the real from them, and in their coherence there with one another, form the only world there is. As I have said elsewhere: "Language—our first formal system—has the sinews of our bodies, which had them first; . . . the grammar, the syntax, the ingenuous choreography of our rhetorical engagement with the world . . . are preformed in that of our prelingual mindbodily being in the world."

If this be granted, then neither the language of science nor the language of poetry may be said to enjoy *a context-neutral* privilege as the vector of the nature of things or to participate less than fully in the formation and articulation of the *only* world in which we live and move and have our being—which is to say, outrageous though it sounds in the setting of 350 years of modern dualism, *the only world there is.* The scandal disappears when we recognize that this has been a long season of self-alienating madness, that a form of discourse—

[a]See *A Philosophical Daybook*, pp. 59f, Appendix, pp. 195–203.

gesture, dance, ordinary language, song, stories, pure mathematics—that does not have its origin in and continually retrotend the primordial ordinations of our lively convivial mindbodily sentience, motility, and orientation is *strictly unimaginable* and would be quite beyond our comprehension, and that none is less a vector of the real than any other.

6/1/90

When I reflect upon the logos that, throughout, enforms the sentience, motility, and orientation of my lively mindbody it will appear in very different articulate forms according to whether the focus of my reflection is a gesture, a string quartet, a sonnet, a narrative, an oration, a computation, logical inference, or mathematical heuristics. I shall be struck by the *disanalogies* among these cases—so potently indeed that the sense of a common logos ordering them all will only barely force itself upon me.

But an *analogy* does indeed hold among them. The logic of all these forms (and all other appearances of meaning as well) derives from and never ceases to retrotend the arché of the integral mindbody through which I am—we are—convivially worlded. Here the forms are indwelt, apprehended, and made into a coherent world that is at once dynamic and changeful, yet stable.

As romanticism sought to cultivate and sublime a form of discourse in which to disclose and preserve uniquely human realities—the reality of value, of spirit, of a world- transcending unification of the self in Being—it siezed upon the *disanalogies* among the ways in which logos asseverates itself in, say, the composition of a tragedy or a fugue or even in the formation of a genetic theory and the discovery of the double helix, on one hand, and that which appears in our reversible hence explicitable acts of formal, reversible ratiocination, on the other.

In doing this romanticism was able to claim "imagination" as a countervailing reality to the Enlightenment's regnant intellectualism, but in such a way as to fail to see that our so- called creative powers are continuous with our exercise of instrumental reason, since they have the same provenance and authority in the hierarchy of existential modalities of our convivial mindbodies in the world. Therefore myths, stories, histories, eschatologies, sense experience, neuroanatomy, astrophysics, and the theory of sets in which we dwell—sometimes alternately, sometimes simultaneously—all enter into the cohering world brought forth and endorsed by our convivial mindbodies; and hence none of these forms, nor others like them, can enjoy any *context-neutral* privilege as a vector of the real.

6/4/90

Poetry, were it to be seen in this light, would have a standing such as it has not had since Plato banished the poets from his ideal republic.

As the formation of human sensibility became more and more comprehensively to be the work of literacy; and therefore men and women came "naturally" to see and evaluate their own reality from the perspective of the new "objectivity"—from the standpoint, namely, of our sun, abstracted from our earthly home by Copernicanism, that is, "freed" for putatively unencumbered intellection from the moil of our concrete existence in time; from the point of view, as well, of the static, "eternal" printed or chirographic word as standard of meaning, value, and truth in the new universe of print—the life-world of oral-aural humankind, for whom the characteristically human-making acts of speaking and hearing speech amidst their quotidian doings are definitive, came to be displaced.

Let us put this in another way. As logos became affiliated with the chirographic word, bringing forth thereby a new conception of truth, value, and reality, since the latter, being static and "eternal," was not, as a vector, subject to the chances and changes of oral-aural memory, *epos* (once the lexical twin of logos), namely, narrative speech, the rhapsodic telling of tales and the oral-aural reciprocities of everyday life (in which we find ourselves as actual speakers and hearers of words, convivially at the dynamic center of a world distended, as we are, in time) began its millennial recession to a secondary and then a tertiary role as bearer of meaning.

Poetry thus has in its context a legitimacy of *equal primacy with all other vectors of reality;* it is an instrument of research[b] and world formation when speech and the uptaking of speech—which even in these latter days we have not ceased to practice—are accorded the de jure authority that they could not fail de facto to exercise in our ordinary doings and sayings.

Thus, in banishing the poets, Plato—and indeed, philosophy in general, that creature par excellence of literacy—banished the reality of oral-aural man, even though this banishment was not fully achieved for some 2000 years.

Cartesianism is the fulfillment of the historical movement from orality to literacy, bringing with it the ultimate form of human self-estrangement: a universe

---

[b]Elizabeth Sewell.

embodied in mathematical discourse in the formal elements of which there are no egocentric particulars for making explicit references to specific times and places in the actual world, no tenses for expressing the temporal distension and deployment in time of such a world, no demonstrative or personal pronouns.

At the very moment of this denouement, Pascal, the first and greatest of postmodern men asks: "What is a man in the infinite?"

6/5/90

In the 325 years or so since this question was first posed there has hardly been an answer that has not suffered from an inherent instability wrought by the contradictions between, on one hand, the epistemological, ontological, and rhetorical values introjected from our literacy and borne by our formal and casual, our explicit and tacit philosophical accounts of ourselves; and those, of orality, on the other hand, that, though in theory subordinate to the former, have of course persisted in the daily practice of our quotidian life of speaking and hearing speech.

This contradiction cuts deep and can be overcome only by going deeper, by producing a new Copernican revolution, making good on the aborted Kantian one, that is, by going all the way past the dualism of epistemological subject and noetic object to the roots and arché of *all* sense reading, all meaning and meaning discernment that is given in the unreflected intentionalities of our convivial mindbodily sentience, motility and orientation.

The context in which this outrageous claim can be seen to achieve some plausibility is in the extended colloquy—it is no "argument" in any sense familiar to the philosophical tradition—that is to be found in *Polanyian Meditations: In Search of a Post-Critical Logic* and *A Philosophical Daybook: Post-Critical Investigations*, which are herewith incorporated by reference into these reflections.

6/7/90

What does T. S. Eliot mean when, in *Burnt Norton*, he says: "[Words] Decay with imprecision, will not stay in place / Will not stay still"?

This is not the judgment that a particular form of words is imprecise: "Well, that puts the case rather imprecisely; we need rather to say . . . Whatever it is that is finally taken "to be the case" is something at which you and I will have arrived by a series of what we agree are approximations to a degree of precision that we finally accept as "precise enough." And that is a question that has no sense except in a particular context. But "Words decay with imprecision": This seems to be a statement about every conceivable state of affairs and the bearing upon them of every conceivable set of forms of words. This is obviously language "on holiday." Although it appears to be doing heavy work, it in fact has no traction: a steering wheel connected to no wheels on the road.

What does it mean to say, "Language always lies"? To begin with, this proposition must be "true" of the proposition "Language always lies," in which case "Language always lies" is a lie; or if it is not "true" of it, not applicable, then sometimes language tells the truth . . . etc. It is as impossible for language always to lie as it is for every single person always to lie. Clearly, some more language on holiday.

What is the impulse behind the utterance of these sweeping, empty claims? Gnosticism: A pathos born of the sense that spirit has fallen into the prison-house of language, from which the only escape is its systematic dismantling by means of a doctrine of aporia, the radical undecidability of the meaning of words.

The cost of this reprieve is the nihilism that is often the flip side of gnosticism.

Undecidability as to the meaning of a word is resolved by a simple *decision*—namely, an assertion—with which our days are filled by the hundreds of thousands. Is the meaning of the words in which sponsors of the doctrine of undecidability speak undecidable?

It is just here that the triviality of most poststructuralist literary theory and criticism lies. One of its suppressed premises is that language is not only a unique, but the sole vehicle of meaning—in which role it notoriously fails because of aporia—that it is to be examined in inert texts, abstracted from its use in speaking and hearing speech, withdrawn from the lively, convivial, mindbodily exchanges of the oral-aural setting. Therefore it is blind to the resolution of undecidability by acts of assertion. It is truly Cartesianism in extremis.

6/14/90

The gravamen of de Man's critique of Heidegger's exegesis of Hölderlin is that, contrary to Heidegger's claim that the poet speaks Being, he cannot do so since the very language that he is required to use shatters all immediacy, in which Being must abide. Poetry cannot "establish the absolute presence of Being"; it can at most embody a longing for it.

This phrase is the fulcrum of the critique. It is also here that its irrelevance is manifest, for we must wonder whether the phrase is in any way applicable to what Heidegger means by *Sein* (*"Sein heisst Beständigkeit im Anwessenheit"*—Being is steadfastness in presence).

We must however bracket the philological debate in favor of doing a deconstruction upon de Man's phrase in itself, since cognate phrases and animadversions upon the concept 'presence' are the materials out of which much deconstructionist polemic is fashioned.

What is the imaginative context out of which the phrase, "absolute presence of Being" emerges; with what suppressed models and analogies is the concept 'immediacy' being used?

The superordinate epistemological paradigms of our philosophical tradition are drawn from our second-order representations of sight, not the dynamic actuality of our visual explorations of the visible. We are even more likely in referring to this sense to use an abstract, therefore static, noun such as *sight* in preference to the gerund *seeing,* which would preserve something of the dynamic actuality of our experience.

Sight, this reflected derivative of our actual experience as seers, is made superordinate over our other senses, is depicted as "taking place" in a dead slice of visual space without temporal thickness—in "eternity," in other words, is for this reason the "experiential" source of our contrast between eternity (simultaneity, *totum simul*) and time,[c] and a model (the deconstructionists say the dominant one) for "presence" and for "immediacy." We have introjected the images and values of our literacy, our imaginations now subject to the sua-

---

[c]See pp. 57ff., *Polanyian Meditations.*

sions of the static chirographic or printed word in preference to the dynamism of the spoken and heard word.

This sense of presence Derrida imputes, rightly, to the whole philosophic tradition and so energetically exposes in his assault upon the "transcendental unity of consciousness" of Husserl.

Having accomplished this exposé, Derrida (and de Man, not to speak of their lesser followers) mounts the whole deconstructionist assault upon meaning, believing that language has slipped its bonds and now hangs in midair, since *presence,* its erstwhile anchor, has given way—or has never existed.

This conception of presence is a highly parochial one, derived as it is from the superordination of sight as an epistemological paradigm, and does not even reckon with the manifold different senses of *presence* in ordinary language, which various uses are far from being without philosophical import.

The whole deconstructionist program is carried out subject to the afterimage of *presence*—understood in this way: a 180° turn on a fixed axis!

6/19/90

While it is true that de Man does not consistently invoke the phrase *establish the absolute presence of Being* to embody his mortified conception of the Being that everywhere eludes us, it is clear that at this crux in his dispute with Heidegger over Hölderlin's view of the powers of poetry, he has, in this phrase, come to rock bottom in his own imagination. Being would *have* to be, could *only* be that which can appear in all its total simultaneity in a dead slice of visual space—in other words, in "eternity," that is, *immediately,* subject in no wise to mediation, that is to say, to being cut in half (L. L. mediare), suffering no intervention, no interruption wrought by a medium that *comes* between the sundered halves, but also goes between them.

If Being, as de Man chooses to understand it, is immediacy and immediacy is a dead slice of visual space without temporal thickness, then, a fortiori, *no* medium—not language, not music, nothing *conceivable*—can "speak Being" since by definition it cannot suffer any such interruption, mediation. And this of course is exactly as de Man and Derrida would have it.

But this is self-evident! True a priori. Why then do de Man and Derrida, in their different ways, go to exhausting lengths to show that this is so?

Or again. De Man says . . . "sign and meaning can never coincide . . ." Taken in a perfectly obvious sense, the statement is plainly false. To say of anything that it is a *sign* is to say that it has a meaning; to say of anything that it has a *meaning,* is to say that it is a sign. *Sign* and *meaning* regularly and *necessarily* coincide since they are coimplicates of one another. De Man must have something else in mind.

What more then is being called for? I suggest that when de Man says this he is wishing for (what he knows he cannot have), such a coincidence as could appear in the immediacy of a dead slice of visual space without temporal thickness (that, as we have seen, derives from the superordination of images drawn from our accounts of seeing as epistemological models) where sign and meaning *perfectly* and *necessarily* coincide and are therefore indistinguishable.

Why does a critic of de Man's acuity belabor the self-evident? I suggest it is because a hidden agendum is at work. He trades heavily upon the impossibility of mediating immediacy, of speaking Being, of representing unity or the unification of our experience when immediacy, Being, and unity are envisaged in the way I have claimed he does. His certainty of *this* impossibility places him, so he tacitly imagines, beyond the aesthetic temptations of every conceivable mode of immediacy, Being, and unity (or, more accurately, conceiving of Being, immediacy and presence in *this* way prevents his conceiving of alternatives) that, as a "reformed" romantic, an inverted aesthete, he has reason to fear, not least because it led him as a young man into a form of aesthetic nationalism that for a time allowed him to embrace National Socialism.

From so austere a conception of the relation between signs and meaning, of Being, immediacy and the unification of experience it is a very short distance to the rejection of all conceivable alternative models of immediacy, Being, and unity and the avowal of the undecidability of the relation between all signs and all meanings. The whole program still lies in the shadow of presence, so conceived, even after presence, so conceived, has been discredited.

The supreme irony in all of this is of course that the ultimate triumph of aestheticism lies in the embrace *of all these models* of presence, Being, immediacy, and meaning—even as they are being explicitly rejected. The assertion of the absence of presence, *conceived in this way,* with the resulting doctrine of undecidability, places this inquiry as far as it could possibly be from the quotidian, mindbodily world of action and responsibility. In other words, it is aestheticism in the ultimate magnitude. Truly, this is, to use the de Manian idiom, "blindness."

That with which we are left, then, is presence, Being, immediacy, and meaning defined as the *negates* of these unattainable creatures of aestheticism. The critic who would expose all forms of (dangerous) aestheticism is the author of its most esoteric triumph: the absolute *absence* of Being.

6/21/90

The mindbody as imagination can thus be so arrested in its own thoroughly romantic-gnostic image of a pristine Being, importunately making itself present in its *absence,* that it will fail to remark the manifold ways that Being tacitly asseverates its presence as *present* through all the mindbody's convivial quotidian doings and sayings, incarnate in the world.

The late Latin *mediare* means to cut in half. From it come medium, to mediate, mediation.

A medium cuts asunder, interrupts, intervenes upon something that hitherto possesses some kind of wholeness, integrity, coherence. But, as medium, that which sunders, it is at the same time a mediator, referring the sundered parts to one another, doing the work of mediation, acting as a go-between.

A medium as go-between acquires the sense of a vector, a bearer of a relationship between the halves that it has put asunder: it expresses the connection of the one to the other; the meaning of the one for the other; the residual kinship that survives the rupture, as the language employed by a mediator as the medium of mediation between parties to a rupture attests to a common meaning that survives their breach and is in fact at once the conditio sine que non of their rift and its healing.

It is this sense of medium as vector of meaning that is at play when S. K. says that only the music of *Don Giovanni* can be the medium of demonic eroticism. This sense also is at work when we say that oil is the medium of Velasquez's *Las Maniñas* and marble the medium of Michelangelo's *David.*

The immediate, immediacy, then, refer to a whole, a coherence, a totality that *as such* suffers no interruption, sundering in half or intervention. One might suppose that that image of immediacy is most perfect that logically *could* not suffer any invasion of mediation, any disruption. This would of course be an instant without any temporal thickness in a point without extension. In such a case there is neither spatial nor temporal room for the intervention of even the thinnest medium.

As we saw in the entry for 6/14, it is in our depiction of sight as occurring in a dead slice (that is, one lacking temporal thickness) of visual space in which all the particulars of our visual field are simultaneously copresent, therefore offering no temporal room for the invasion of mediation, that we found a powerful image of immediacy—even if not so pristine as that "in" an instant without temporal thickness "in" a point without extension. It is clear that, in any case, this image that operates powerfully in de Man's imagination leads to his reflections upon the impossibility of mediating Being.

The question needing to be asked is: Are we inextricably bound by this depiction of Being and immediacy?

6/22/90

If Being is conceived in such fashion that it can "exist" only in immediacy, and if immediacy can, at most, be depicted as "existing" beyond time and only in a space that is an abstract, static derivation from our reflected accounts of our actual experience of looking and seeing, it follows that Being cannot be mediated. This proposition is true by definition. Being, so conceived, cannot appear in the world. Can it appear in the world, can immediacy manifest itself in time, if they are rendered by other models?

I do not apprehend the whole formed by the constituent notes of J. S. Bach's First Prelude in C of *The Well-Tempered Clavier* in an instant, a "moment" without temporal thickness—even if an approximation of such an instantaneous apprehension is imaginable in the case of the simultaneous sounding of all the constituent notes. In the latter case, obviously, we are not talking any more of the First Prelude.

If however each note were not engraved upon my attentive and ductile mindbody as it pretended the next note and retrotended its predecessor, there to be husbanded in the tonus of my lively mindbody, deeply implicated in the web of its intentionalities as it exists in its own worldly temporal setting, then it could never be the case that I should "hear" the First Prelude. Its first note and its last note have to be copresent with one another within a temporal coherence that is given in the mindbody upon which they have been engraved. Were this not the case I should not apprehend the totality of the prelude when it is done. *Since* this is so, the coherence, the immediacy—the absence of all interventions upon it—that the First Prelude is perceived to have, the resolution of all the tensions that are embodied in its constituent notes unfolding in time, that the completed piece of music achieves, is but one side of a reality the other side of which is the resolution, coherence, and immediacy that I experience at that moment in my mindbodily life. Immediacy has been mediated in time by the medium of the notes resounding in the tonus of my mindbody. And Being, insofar as it is affiliated with immediacy, has, as well, been mediated in the world.

Unless I am mistaken, this is at a great remove from Heidegger's sense of *Sein.* Nevertheless there is a strong sense in which Being, so conceived, merits the characterization of *Beständigkeit im Anwessenheit;* and if we dismiss it out of hand, it is for no other reason than the fact that we are immured in our disappointment at the loss of a logically *impossible* conception of Being and immediacy for which no merely *possible* one can be a substitute, since it is only from the standpoint of the presence as absent of this impossible immediate Being that the putative deficiencies of Being that actually appears in the world are asserted or assumed.

Being, absolute presence, immediacy are defined as without temporal thickness or spatial extension, statically beyond the conditions of existence in the world; therefore, by definition, beyond the possibility of mediation. Yet do we not need to wonder what the preceding language is accomplishing; whether through it we are being given access to "absolute presence" in declaring of it what we presumably "know" as we speak of its unknowabilty. Is it not being "mediated" precisely in our declarations of its unmediability? Does it not by these means truly make an appearance in the world? If this is the case, then de Man's and Derrida's critiques of all claims of access to presence in the Western philosophic tradition in this sense are in fact *often a mediation of this presence* that they are at pains to declare cannot be done! Indeed, both declarations of the accessibility of absolute Being and declarations of its inaccessibility have precisely the same ground: our mindbodies in their sentience, motility, and orientation in the world from which all explorations of the real emanate and in which they cohere to form the world.

6/25/90

The distinction I have drawn previously between the presence, immediacy, and Being that can be shown to appear in the First Prelude, on one hand, and that which I claim cannot be mediated *in time,* since, by definition, it "exists" in a dead slice of visual space in "eternity," on the other, still trades upon an old dualism, as do de Man and Derrida.

I am most faithful to my own thought when I recognize that, although the definition of an extramundane realm of truth and meaning entails that it will lie outside the realm of becoming and to such an extent is the conception of a reality that cannot be "mediated in time," it is even so, a conception derived from my mindbody, itself fully incarnate in the world of time; and therefore, *as my conception,* it is necessarily mediated in time[d]—as I try to suggest in my previous question: Is not "absolute presence" being mediated precisely in our declaration of its unmediability? I believe no such *ontological* dualism between the temporal world in which I live and move and have my being and an eternal realm is tenable. Even "the eternal realm" is subject to the temporality of the world in which it appears in conception.

I do not draw from this the conclusion that de Man and Derrida seem to draw: There being no *extramundane* realm of truth, meaning, presence, or Being, there can *be*

---

[d]See *A Philosophical Daybook,* p. 70.

none of these *in time,* so that all is finally left in a state of undecidability in the world.

Of course, any argument that can show that immediacy, absolute presence, Being and meaning through the use of the First Prelude as their medium, can a fortiori make the same case with J. S. Bach's *St. Matthew Passion* or *A Musical Offering,* infinitely more complex in structure and more extended in time though they are, and therefore requiring a greater span of attention.

6/26/90

When I say, as earlier, that no *ontological* dualism between the temporal world in which I live and move and have my being, on one hand, and an eternal realm—obviously outside time—on the other, what do I mean? What does it mean to say that the conception of an extramundane realm of meaning and truth that, by definition, cannot be mediated in time, must *necessarily* be mediated in time inasmuch as such a conception is formulated by taking the negate of those qualities that characterize embodiments of meaning and Being in the ordinary world (e.g., atemporal, aspatial) and imputing them to such a realm?

It is to remind myself of what I deeply believe: My lively, sentient, motile, oriented mindbody, ensconced in the temporality of the ordinary world of its doings and sayings is absolutely radical, whence the whole texture and weave of the world is given definition; therefore it is the omnipresent, inalienable, logically necessary matrix within which all my acts of meaning discernment are conceived and brought to term, no matter how abstracted from this matrix are the vectors by which these acts are borne.

However thinly prescinded from my quotidian world may be my pretensive mindbodily explorations of the real, however rarified become the vectors of these inquiries, they never cease to retrotend this matrix that is their ontological-logical ground. It is in this sense that there is at bedrock—since bedrock is my integral mindbody—no "ontological" dualism of an extramundane realm of "absolute presence of Being" and the world in which I live and move and have my being. All come to ground and derive not just their authority, but their very intelligibility in my mindbody. Whatever proximate uses the distinction between the world and the extramundane may have—and they are many—it cannot be ultimate. Both the *concept* of an extramundane realm and the *extramundane realm* to which the concept refers are in—and *equally* in—the world.

Does this then mean that there can be nothing that transcends the world? No, it does not. My every act of speech, insofar as I novelly own and own up to it, transcends the world.[e]

The disanalogies that hold between J. S. Bach's First Prelude in C and a Shakespearean sonnet, let us say number 73, the first line of which is "That time of year thou mayest me behold . . ." are many and patent. It is not however necessary to make an exhaustive catalogue of these before remarking the overpowering analogy between them. By means of the notes of the prelude and the words of the sonnet, there is engraved upon my attentive mindbody, distended in time, a coherence, meaning, Being, and temporal immediacy—there are no interventions upon it, no invasion of its totality in a certain finite

[e]Cf. *A Philosophical Daybook,* pp. 29, 95–96; *Polanyian Meditations,* pp. 95, 126–29.

time—are mediated. One side of the resolution thus achieved is in the prelude and the sonnet; its other side is my mindbody, itself, too, a medium of this mediation of Being.

Seen in this light, Bach's music and Shakespeare's poetry do not reach out for Being and tragically fail. They mediate it in the midst of the most ordinary textures of the mindbodily life of their hearers.

6/27/90

In the *Timaeus* Plato says: "Time is the moving image of eternity." I take him to mean that inasmuch as time *moves* it is a *mere* image (not the thing itself) of eternity, "wherein" there is no change nor shadow that is caused by turning, and that it nevertheless is a real *image* of eternity, inasmuch as time moves in a circular fashion: It moves *rhythmically,* the form of movement that, in contrast to chaotic, that is, irrational, movement, approaches absolute stasis.

If we imagine a circle every point on the circumference of which is equidistant from its geometric center, a point without spatial or temporal extension, we can then go on to imagine its circumference contracting until every point on it, all being equidistant from the center, will be "assimilated" to that center which is, as we have stipulated, a point without spatial or temporal extension. This point is the Platonic model of the form of the good, of the absolute presence of Being, of immediacy, to which the philosopher may have access through an intellectual intuition at the far side of the exhaustion of the powers of dialectic.

This is the doctrine of absolute presence, allowing for its expression in many different philosophical styles, that has persisted in the whole tradition since Plato and has been attacked by Derrida et al. as beyond access and impossible of mediation.

One of the things I have shown already is that Bach's prelude and Shakespeare's sonnet do in fact mediate Being, absolute presence, immediacy, meaning, value, and so forth in a way analogous to that in which time (as an image) mediates eternity for Plato, albeit for me this "eternity" is derivative of and continually depends upon my mindbody, pretensively and retrotensively in time, and is therefore axiologically subordinate to the latter.

By implication I have also shown that this so-called Western philosophical doctrine of absolute presence is parochial inasmuch as coeval with the rise and dissemination of alphabetic literacy, even though we remain residually oral-aural and even still live our lives in terms of *its* images and values some of the time.

In the light of these discoveries we are able to see that the prelude and the sonnet are *real* mediations of absolute presence and that the Derridian, de Manian critique is fixated upon the afterimage of absolute presence in the Platonic or Husserlian sense.

Is there then some other force for the concepts Being or being—or reality—for me (I believe I fairly consistently capitalize Being only when I wish to call attention to my global sense of the inconceivability of my nonexistence insofar as I dwell in my mindbody in the world as the omnipresent, inalienable, logically-ontologically necessary matrix of all meaning and meaning discernment—upon which, of course, I incessantly and acritically rely as I go about making sense of things amidst my quotidian doings and sayings)?

In addition to there being for me manifold encounters with presence, immediacy, resolution, Being in the fabric of my mindbodily life, there is an ubiquitous experience of encounter with an intractability in this fabric: the pretensions and retrotensions of my mindbody in its transactions with the world—pretensions and retrotensions that lie well below the surface of reflective life, beyond the suasions of volition—operative intentions, as Husserl called them; as well as all that these pretensions and retrotensions themselves encounter as intractable. Only if these intentions were taken as creatures of the "mind," subject to the "will," could this view be construed as a form of idealism. If the world and its epistemological ground are to be depicted as dynamic, these pretensions and retrotensions will have to be taken as *radical;* reflected intentions are derived. My mindbody is for me—our convivial mindbodies are for us—the paradigm of reality; all authority for the uses of *Being, being,* and *real* descends from it.

This reality, as intractable as can be, does not appear in reflection, yet is always manifest at reflection's back, continuously asseverating itself in all our quotidian doings and sayings.

6/28/90

Kierkegaard, through his pseudonymous author, A, in "The Immediate Stages of the musical Erotic," says "Don Giovanni is the absolutely musical idea. . . . He does not have existence at all, but hurries in a perpetual vanishing, precisely, like music." He also says that what one hears in the music of the opera *Don Giovanni* is "restlessness, tumult and infinity."

How can I at once use the word *immediate* to designate what is mediated through the medium of Bach's prelude (that accomplishes this precisely in the resolution, coherence, immediacy, and Being that is engraved upon my attentive mindbody when, unfolding in time, a conclusion is reached, closure established) and to designate the character of Don Giovanni's form of eroticism as this is uniquely mediated through the music of the opera—*this* music that, for S. K., realized the special *genius* of music for expressing "restlessness, tumult and infinity," thereby to be the perfect medium for demonic eroticism? How, in other words, can I say that the opera, and in particular the Champagne Aria sung by Don Giovanni at the banquet, embodies immediacy no less than Bach's First Prelude, even though, as music, the two seem utterly different?

To justify this usage it is necessary to return to my reflections on the etymology of *medium, mediate, immediate.* The late Latin root is *mediare,* to cut in half, to interrupt, to intervene upon.

The *immediacy* in the music of the opera is its restless forward surge—not toward a telos in resolution and closure, as with the Bach; its hurrying in a perpetual vanishing toward—what?—infinity and restlessness! And in doing so, nothing interrupts, nothing intervenes upon its effervescence. A spiritually driven, unbounded, infinitizing—which is to say demonic—eroticism cannot be mediated in language because its movement in time is therein continuously interrupted, intervened upon—cut in half, if you will—by its bonding to the world through its semantic dimension—by egocentric particulars, demonstrative pronouns and, in short, the entire repertoire of formal resources possessed by language and absent from music, preeminently from music that expresses "restlessness, tumult and infinity."

7/3/90

The real world (as to the nature of which only narrowly ecumenic questions are asked until literacy gives rise to criticism), given its first configuration in the mute axioms of significance, the *ur*pretensions to sense and meaning, the as-yet-unreflected logos embodied in the primitive sentience, motility, and orientation of my lively mindbody, makes its decisive appearance when it is called into existence for reflection in the abounding modes of discourse that my mindbody has, in its coition with the world, devised and made to cohere in itself as the world in which I live and move and have my being.

In the texture of this quotidian life, in my doings and sayings in its midst, there is no *bedrock* dualism between myself and the world, between what appears in my discourse as the world and a world that is independent of my discourse; no dualism between subject and object, between sign and signified; no dualism at the radix of my mindbodily being between ontological ground and ontological consequent—their relation being always inherently dialectical.

Distinctions between the members of these pairs—and of course of many others as well—have been indispensable in the philosophical tradition, and even in our commonsense talk. But the *dualisms* are derivative, issuing in fact from the superordination and subliming of the values of literacy over those of the oral-aural matrix in which our ordinary doings and sayings occur and still—even so—command authority over us.

Indeed, these literacy values, that in due course endow us with the prodigious powers of science and technology, as they have become comprehensively privileged, have in our reflective life dimmed to the point of invisibility the values that enform our ordinary doings and sayings.

In the world in which I live and move and have my being, myth and poetry are no less authoritative vectors of the real than are common sense, astrophysics, or pure mathematics—though obviously in a given context one will have more propriety than another.

For all the triumphs of literacy and hence, in due course, of science and technology—and contrary to the 350 year old dogma—the evaluations and notices that tacitly enform the world in which we live and move and have our being still have superordinate authority in that life.

As I write this down I find myself thinking, How can you believe this?—so heavy upon me is the weight of the dogma.

This is the context in which I must perform a deconstruction upon Paul de Man's asseveration's concerning the powers and limitations of poetry as a medium of access to aspects of the real.

In the *Rhetoric of Romanticism* de Man says:

> Poetic language can do nothing but originate anew over and over again [The assumption here being of course that, if poetry fails to grasp without violation the "absolute presence of being" (that is, a totality that exists eternally in a point without spatial or temporal extension), it grasps what only fugitively appears in time and therefore cannot be the vector of the real], it is always *constitutive,* able to *posit* regardless of presence [Does this mean regardless of the absence of presence?] but by the same token, unable to give *a foundation* to what it posits as an intent of consciousness. (my emphasis)

We do not need to know de Man's views concerning the "metaphysical" reach of the language of science or even his views as to whether the language of common sense "only posits as an intent of consciousness, unable to give a foundation to what (commonsense) posits." We do not even need to know de Man's view as to the efficacy to its task of the language in which de Man has asserted, presumably as true, the previous view as to the limits of poetry. In due course, we can, without the benefit of this information, get some clue, by examining the internal logic of de Man's remark, assuming that he meant it, as to the conditions of the possibility of his making it.

At this juncture we need observe only that the remark trades uncritically upon the assumption that the language of poetry is peculiarly equivocal; that the belief among the romantics that poetry could embody Being, immediacy, presence and a unification of experience was an act of hubris.

Ignoring for the moment the merits of these assumptions, we can simply say that in the distinctions between what is (merely) *constituted* and what is not, between what is said to be merely *posited* because no foundation is *given* and what is *not,* in that sense, *posited,* because it is *possessed* of a foundation, we encounter one of the expressions of dualism that was contrived 2600 years ago with the advent of literacy and the substitution of philosophy (epistéme) for poetry (épos).

7/5/90

It would appear from the preceding that, for de Man, the disenchanted and repentant romantic, poetry can be neither about Being, as absolute presence, nor about reality. It cannot "speak Being" (Heidegger's phrase) because "language (while) capable of origination" can never achieve "the absolute identity with itself that exists in the natural object." (Each of the possible constructions of this remark seems to be a tautology that would surprise no one.) It cannot therefore speak Being since Being would *have* to be (is by definition) "absolute presence," indeed, *totum simul.* It cannot be about reality since it is without semantic reach, is only about itself—like music, understood in a certain way—for it conjures up a theoretically infinite number of fugitive worlds with no foundation except an intent of consciousness.

I, on the other hand, hold that Being asseverates itself in a thousand ways in the fabric of our quotidian life, even in poetry in a special way—as I argue above with reference to Shakespeare's Sonnet 73. At the same time, I hold that poetry—and, indeed, music—are two of the modes of discourse that my mindbodily coition with the world has devised and made to cohere in itself as the *real world* in which I live and move and have my being.

The real world for me—convivially, for us—is that which is made to appear in our midst in whose midst we appear, by means of these modes of discourse.

7/6/90

One of Being's asseverations of itself may be seen in de Man's use of expressions such as: "Poetic language . . . is always (merely) constitutive, able to posit . . . (but) unable to give a foundation to what it posits except as an intent of consciousness."

If the language, '(merely) constitutive' and 'able to posit', are to have meaning to de Man as he writes it down, it cannot merely reside in a discarnate mind, in consciousness, but will have had to gain traction within the sinews of his mindbody—the matrix for him of *all* meaning and meaning discernment, this bedrock hermeneutical instrument, the specific existential radix with which all his apprehensions of any sort whatsoever are inextricably implicated. This lively, integral, sentient, motile, and oriented mindbody is necessarily present to his own words when he comprehendingly reads them as it had been when he wrote them down.

For him to grasp in this matrix the exact existential and assertorial weight of *constitute* and *posit* will be for him to apprehend a contrast, *mindbodily given,* between the obstinacy and pertinacity of that Being the nonexistence of which is, in that instant, inconceivable, namely, *his own being* in the world (in no wise exhibiting only the equivocal existence of the merely "posited" or "constituted") and all else that by contrast with his own is deficient in Being.

Of this Being we are not likely to use the predicates *absolute presence of Being* as this language is used by de Man. We can say however that Being asseverates itself in the temporal distension of de Man's mindbodily being in the world, else he could not have said what he said. If this is both true and philosophically weighty, as I believe it to be, then de Man's whole aesthetic is dealt a mortal blow.

Descartes claimed to have certainty of his own existence in his "I think." This certainty in fact had a more primitive root. This he discovered when he imagined "some deceiver, very powerful and very cunning, who is constantly employing his ingenuity in deceiving me."

If I am but a creature in the imagination of such a deceiver—the argument is—then I am only an *imaginary,* that is a merely *constituted, posited* being. If a Being the nonexistence of which is inconceivable, namely my *own* existence in the world, does not asseverate itself, declaring its exemption from the imagination of the deceiver, thereby grounding the distinction between *real* existence and mere imaginary, that is, posited existence, thereby arresting an infinite regress, then I shall be able to entertain no doubts whatever as to the *existence* of anything.

7/10/90

We can discover an even more rarified illustration of the way in which Being—or being, or existence, these can, for my purposes, often be used interchangeably, and can be here—ubiquitously asseverates itself, even in our very act of seeking to bracket it, a la Husserl.

It is quite impossible to bracket the question of the existence—as opposed to the (mere?) appearance—of the transcendental subject as Husserl proposed to do in order to arrive at a presuppositionless foundation for philosophical science.

In the act of affirming in my thought the transcendental subject and, as I do so, tacitly imputing to it as the accusative of that thought the kind of "existence" that it has as this accusative, even as I also am tacitly putting the "existential question out of play," my act of affirmation implies, *is* grounded in, asseverates *my* actual existence in the most ordinary way. The existential question cannot—except in the most abstract, merely conceptual sense—be put out of play. At every level, existence is being asseverated, even as the question of existence is being declared to be out of play; indeed, as the *condition* of doing so.

Derrida's attack upon Husserl's "transcendental subjectivity" is well placed. The angle from which he has come to it, however, enables him to miss entirely the existential import of the very words by means of which he conducts it and to see how the assertion of his every word systematically gives the lie to his doctrine of the undecidability of the meaning of words.

I have held that our concepts have not descended fully formed from heaven, but could have arisen only as figures of its own devising from the mindbody's coition with the world; that they constitute all the usages that enable us to define our situation, recognize who and where we are, to name and appraise the nature of things as being thus and so and not otherwise; and that these concepts will include not only words, but a whole range of our wonted gestures—the thumbs-up sign, the salute, the beckoning finger, the V-for-victory, even our postures.

We have seen, for example, how the not *strictly* conceivable concept of absolute contingency is embedded in the experience that each of us has of being the sole owner, as we speak them, of the words we speak in our own name. If in reflection, we prescind from that experience the element of the *radical underivability* of our words, we arrive at an approximation of a concept of absolute contingency—compromised only by the fact that 'underivability' is parasitical upon 'the derived' as that to which it is oppugnant.

The existential provenance of the concept 'unique' is the experience we each alone have of a relation to our mindbodily existence. This experience achieves its sharpest focus in our every authentic act of speech. This is the very paradigm use of *uniqueness* from which all uses of it descend; it is also the paradigm of the concrete by which all uses of *concrete* are authorized.

When I use the pronoun *I* with the reflexive force it always has when in use I am not merely making an identifying reference to an entity—though no doubt this is accomplished. Nor am I merely identifying myself as over against *you, them, this* (physical object); nor, even the bearer of the proper name *William H. Poteat.* In saying *I,* I assume responsibility. The reflexivity of this pronoun when I use it of myself (it is gratuitous to add *of myself* here since when I *use I* it is always necessarily "of myself") refers back upon me the whole burden of my speech-act and the world that it makes appear between us. *The imputing and bearing of responsibility is implicated in the very grammar of this pronoun in use.*

Of course I could not even *mention* (as opposed to *use*) the pronoun *I* except were I possessed of the full pronominal repertoire of my native language. More to the point here however is the fact that I could not truly *say I* in good faith, thereby, inter alia, accepting responsibility for myself, without being *before* another, a *you,* hearing and taking up what I say. This, too, is implicated in the grammar of the pronouns—*I* is without meaning without *you.* Every speech act is the act of entering into an implied contract, into a covenant with a speech community the conditions—the requirements, terms—of which are given in the grammar of the language.

The darkest image of terror I can conceive is that of my shouting "I am William Poteat," like the figure in Edvard Munch's *The Scream,* into an infinite and infinitely silent universe in which there is no possibility of an answer from either God or man. For here my demand for an answering voice that cannot come, a demand as natural to the act of speaking as the pronominal distinctions themselves, because connate with them, reveals the horror of the *truly* empty word.

This is really the pass to which we are brought by the poststructuralists' doctrine of the undecidability of the meaning of words. If they spoke in good faith, this is where they would arrive. But then, if they spoke in good faith, they would cease to speak.

7/13/90

In common with most philosophers in the Western tradition the poststructuralists have conducted their investigations in the theater of solitude: Reflection and its objects have a fantasy setting in which the thinker contemplates the objects of thought in solitude, after the fashion of a solitary reader silently beholding the inert words upon the printed page—a very different theater of reflection than one fashioned upon our experience in the lively reciprocity of the oral-aural setting. The products of their investigations are therefore static, even though the subjects of these inquiries are in actuality—in, that is to say, the warp and woof of our ordinary doings and sayings—dynamic.

Poststructuralists have therefore been inclined to hold that there can be no embodiment in time and language of an absolutely present Being, since language fractures the immediacy that Being, so conceived, must preserve—a tautology, as we have seen.

As the complement to this doctrine they have held that no absolutely present self can abide in time, since, like Being, it would also have to "exist" in a dead slice of visual space as conceived in the theater of solitude. All this is taken to be apodictic.

From this latter doctrine they have inferred that literature can have no certainly identifiable voice, that the reader before it can have only a fugitive being; indeed, with consummate silliness but perfect consistency, that the text can have no author, he? or she? or it?—how can we now say this?—being replaced by "a mobile army of tropes and metaphors."[f]

But selfhood is an "ethical" category, as we have already begun to see in analyzing the implications embodied by the logical grammar of the pronoun *I* in use. We may even come to see that selfhood is an ethico-religious category.

The self is not a "sensation" like warm or red—as Hume professed to be dismayed to discover; it is not a "notion" that Berkeley thought could countervail Hume's reductive sensationalism; it is not the *cogito,* not consciousness over against its objects; it is not Kant's transcendental unity of apperception, wherein all experience is apprehended as unified in "I think" nor is it just that unification wrought in my apprehension of the moral law—although this proposal has the enormous advantage of seeing the self as subject to responsibility and therefore required to act; it is not transcendental subjectivity (Husserl), safely prescinded from the empirical self; it is not a concrescence of prehensions (Whitehead)—although such language succeeds in representing it as dynamic ("a concrescing of prehendings" would be better).

None of these contrivances—most of them conceived in the theater of solitude—can succeed, quite simply because the self's existence is covenantal and therefore can be entertained only in a theater of reflection that derives its stage setting from the convivial world of speaking and hearing speech where *in these very acts* and in the grammar of the language in which they are per-

[f]Lindsey Waters in *Paul de Man: Critical Writings 1953–1978,* p. xxxi.

formed implied contracts are continually being negotiated.

7/16/90

Truly covenantal speech is possible only when a speaker and a hearer, who speaks in turn, are perceived and perceive themselves as appearing before one another in the actual speaking of the absolutely novel words of which they are the unique authors and owners; whose words are therefore not "natural," that is to say, that, however necessarily they must transcend *from* the world, they cannot be *reduced to* it, conceptually comprehended in it. In thus mutually appearing we transcend the world and even ourselves, insofar as we are taken to be mere items in an inventory of nature: we are therefore spirits. (At this remark, laboring under the burden of my lifelong commitment to the values and models that I have introjected from my literate culture, I can barely resist saying: "Is *that all* that spirit is—the most insubstantial thing imaginable, only the breath, vanishing into thin air?)

So conceived, the speakers in a Platonic dialogue—whatever else may have been the case as they went about their ordinary affairs in the Agora—could not have been perceived nor have perceived themselves as engaged in covenantal speech. *In the terms of the dialogue,* in, that is, the terms of Plato's logos doctrine, their words could not be absolutely novel nor could they be uniquely authored and owned-up to by those who spoke them. *In this setting,* an act of speech would have had to be conceived as an act of *anamnesis* of the eternal logoi. Speech—

covenantal speech—had not yet been vested with its rights.[g]

The exemplary model of covenantal speech in our tradition is in the meeting between Yahweh and Abram.

Yahweh—whose very name, "I will be that I will be," is a covenant—summoned Abram to leave Ur of Chaldees, to foreswear the worship of the moon and of fertility and, in answering the unique, underivable words of a world-transcending God with his own uniquely authored, world-transcending words, to become Abraham, an incarnate spirit, the father of many nations, party to a promise. Before an ultimately inscrutable God, Abraham now apprehends himself as ultimately inscrutable to himself.

And all the reductionism and naturalism of our Enlightenment, though the attrition has been severe, has not evacuated our sense that, in our ordinary oral-aural exchanges we speak and hear our own unique and underivable words, and in owning them, appear to one another in covenant.

If I do not see that the radical truth about my selfhood is that it is covenantal, I will seek it in vain and, finally in despair, in all the preceding philosophical contrivances, everyone of which in its reductionism impoverishes me as spirit. If however I do see it as a covenant, I shall be free to view myself in the light of first one of these and then another, with disinterest, profit and without Angst.

---

[g]If I have drawn the inferences from the Platonic model with what may appear a ludicrous kind of ruthlessness, thereby suggesting a rather daunting picture of ordinary conversation in the Agora or the Stoa of Zeus, it will not be because such has not been licensed by the model.

An aesthetical representation of reality is one in which its beholder is never confronted by "an otherness that can say I,"[h] which inert words upon a printed page assuredly cannot be.

Most of the philosophy of our tradition gives such an aesthetical representation. As the latest version of this aestheticism (in many cases aspiring itself to repudiate aestheticism) poststructuralist literary theory has rightly disavowed, at times it appears for the sake of a liberation, these static contrivances for expressing selfhood. Being however aesthetical, it lacks, as a philosophic resource, the conception of a covenantal self, of selfhood as an ethical category. It can therefore find neither the voice in the text nor the self in the reader. All therefore ends in aporia, in undecidability—ultimately in the abolition of humankind as the unanticipated outcome of liberation.

7/19/90

Why do I feel that the coinage *mindbody* and its cognates—devised for the writing of *Polanyian Meditations* to provide me the means of sustaining my grip upon my central idea and the conceptual footing from which to explore its implications (which critics have found so awkward and uncomfortable that, having said this, they have lapsed immediately into the old, hyphenated form, *mind-body*)—why do I find that there is something equivocal about it as a concept? Why does it seem to make a peculiar demand upon me as I find myself writing it down? Why do I feel that it ought to engage you, the reader, as no other concept does in the text in which it appears? Why indeed is it awkward?

---

[h]W. H. Auden.

I want to suggest that an answer may be found in exploring, the analogies between the role of *I* in our ordinary usage and that of *mindbody* in my various reflections. Perhaps discovering these will also help us in apprehending the force that *mindbody* is designed to have as a means of access to the new mode of dwelling in the world that I have been undertaking to induce.

I is an awkward concept when viewed in terms of its logical grammar.

The words of a language work because of their transferability. Without this, everything in the universe would have to have a proper name.

We can educe the interesting logical peculiarity—awkwardness, if you please—of *I* by comparing its modes of behavior with that of the pronoun *he* and the proper name *William H. Poteat.*

Unlike *William H. Poteat,* which will not be found in the *Oxford English Dictionary* and therefore no part of English, *he* and *I,* which are in the *O.E.D.,* thus parts of English, may be used to refer to any number of particulars, even if when they are actually so used, they are always equivalent to one and only one proper name. *Like* proper names *he* and *I,* on being used, name particular persons. In this respect they are equivalent to proper names. However, unlike proper names they share with other tokens in the language some degree of transferability.

He and *I,* though both parts of the language, do not possess the same degree of transferability. *He* may be used by an indefinite number of people of an indefinite number of people on different occasions, and when used by any given person may mean a different person on every single occasion. *I,* however, even though it is used by an indefinite number of people, can, when *used* by any person, mean only one person on every single occasion that it is used by that person.

This means that *I,* unlike *William H. Poteat,* possesses logical transferability. It is thus a part of language. However, unlike *he* it possesses only minimum transferability. Whenever it is used by a given person, *I* means only one person on every occasion that it is used by that person. In other words, *I, in use,* always functions reflexively. It names the namer, it recoils upon language and its user.

Thus *I* is a transferable token in English like *he* and *the man next door.* But its status in language is unique because uniquely equivocal. For this reason, when it appears in a speech act it continually makes reference to the privileged standing in the world of the author of the constituent words of that act.[i]

As we learned our native language we came quite naturally to understand the rules by which it works, long before we had made an explicit study of grammar. The first personal pronoun singular nominative case, with its unique reflexive force did not strike us as awkward anymore than the other usages into which we came so naturally—although it is of some interest that, generally, we come to use *I* of ourselves last, referring to ourselves until then with the third person or, occasionally, with our proper name. This is doubtless connected with the fact that the elders from whom we learn language refer to us as *you* or *William,* since the limited transferability of *I* makes it impossible for them to use it to refer to anyone but themselves.

[i]Cf., "God and the Private I," *Philosophy and Phenomenological Research* 20, no. 3 (March 1960).

In any case, because we have, in acquiring our language and in using it with unreflected ease, come to take all its demands quite for granted, there is nothing awkward about any of it, even with the logically equivocal first person singular. Yet this token—and this is especially obvious in our oral-aural exchanges—at once reflexively reiterates its partially extralinguistic status and systematically alludes to the extralinguistic, existential actuality of my mindbodily being in the world, which is the omnipresent background and footing in the actual for the largely abstract system of language. For example, *this* and *that,* even though they may be said to possess maximum transferability, being applicable to absolutely every single particular in the universe, will always refer to a concrete particular, which office it can perform only by being anchored in the extralinguistic, existential actuality of my mindbodily being as I speak, which is denominated by the reflexivity of the first personal pronoun.

In the *written* text of my argument—as opposed to its viva voce presentation—I often speak in the first person and regularly refer to "my mindbodily being in the world." Here, I try to produce a *reflexive force* for these words as a way to confront you *even in the medium of writing* with my mindbodily self as if I were before you in the commonsense world, *speaking into* the text my existential actuality *for me* in the use of this "reflexive" form. At the same time I want you to read "my mindbodily being in the world" as "*my* (your) mindbodily being," to bring *your* existential reality *for you* into the text you are reading; to issue an invitation to *you* to adopt the position toward your own primordial actuality that is analogous to that you are in when you use the pronoun *I.*

All the foregoing will seem precious only if we forget how our introjection of the values and models of literacy, endorsed and consolidated in every text we read, has estranged us from our mindbodily actuality as it appears in our quotidian oral-aural life. If it is the case, as I hold, that there are no articulations of the nature of things that are not seen ultimately to derive from and refer incessantly to the mute axioms of significance that issue from the sentience, motility, and orientation of the mindbodies that we *first* and *unceasingly* know without mediation as the vectors of our participation in reality, then all argument concerning the nature of things, whether it be in writing or in lively speech, must find ways to reawaken us again and again to that which is closer to us than we are to ourselves; and in which all things—first and last—inhere.

If then my critics have found the coinage *mindbody* awkward, I have succeeded in my goal. As a word designed to have a reflexive force, thereby violating the logico-grammatical surface tension of the text in the hope that the reader may be dragged, against all his or her aculturated impulses, into the text itself, it is meant to be awkward.

7/23/90

In using the expression *my mindbody,* I continually remind myself, against the seductions of this culture, that it is *from* my own immediately actual being in the world that I argue. And I use it, too, to induce you to use 'my mindbody' of yourself as you read in order to remind *you* that it is *to* your immediately actual being that I argue: this to recover what has been lost or obscured by the effects of literacy hypertrophied.

The logos of articulate language is parasitical, as we have seen, upon the mute and unarticulated logos of our sentience, motility, and orientation, which achieves the first forms of distal indication in our gestural life as it moves toward its telos in articulation. Language can never be finally alienated from these mindbodily roots and hence from reality.

However, looked at from the standpoint of the logic of that late arrival upon the scene, articulate language, the first personal pronoun I, with its amphibious status vis-à-vis other verbal forms, binds the abstract system of language to the world by its recurring reminder of its provenance and its present existential ground and authority in the as yet unarticulated.[j]

---

[j]All expression is at once the *real in itself* and the *vectors* of the real. (The words that you have just read both say what I specifically mean in this case and are emergents from the vast lingual background within which I continually dwell, itself alluding to its prelingual ground.) Being, reality, meaning, value asseverate themselves in my every act of speaking and writing, moving and gesturing, singing and dancing. For it is these convivial expressive acts of each of us that together make a world appear.

The very tokens of my speaking—and indeed of all my acts of expression—when viewed from the perspective of the acts through which they appear, body-forth *in themselves* and are the marks of my unmediated participation in Being. So intimate, in other words, is the bond between the *instruments* of our expression and *what* is thereby expressed that no in principle ecumenic skepticism about the adequation of words to the world is possible. In our ordinary talk we may disagree about the appositeness of this word or that—though far less often than we imagine when doing philosophy. But we do not, on this account, entertain serious doubts—in our ordinary colloquies—that what we say is about the world that our talk itself causes to appear.

"Neither the language of science nor the language of poetry may be said to enjoy a *context-neutral* privilege as the vector of the nature of things or to participate less than fully in the formation and articulation of the *only* world in which we live and move and have our being." I read these words over and remember the conviction with which, not long ago, I wrote them down and wonder how this could have been. Something has come between me and them. How do I find my way back to that relation to my being in the world from which this remark came?

Whence the conception of a world? Let us begin with this question. But first, a warning.

7/24/90

As we have seen, the invention and propagation of alphabetic writing set Western men and women free from their "dependence"—as this is viewed from the perspective of the new literacy—upon the chances and changes of oral-aural memory. This not only put at human disposal a powerful new instrument for the investigation into the nature of things; it gave them as well a new way of conceiving their nature; and it provided them with a new

---

When, on the other hand, these words and gestures are regarded from the standpoint of their sedimentation in our midst as the world in which we live and move and have our being, they are the *medium* by which the real, meaning, Being, and value appear.

Thus the power of the logos at the root of my mindbodily coition with its ground asseverates itself in the primal ordinations of my being; in my sentience, motility, and orientation; and at length issues in the very words I speak: *in themselves* tokens of the real; even as just the rational, that is, grammatically and syntactically ordered, vehicles of speech.

repertoire of images, values and models for depicting the nature of themselves in the world. In these men and women came to define themselves as a mind untrammeled by the flux within fugitive time over against a determinate world—the perfect complement to the picture of themselves as a silent reader of the perduring words of a written text.

In this picture of themselves men and women were granted the power to transcend, master and—at least in reflection—neutralize the fugitive, therefore unreal, coming into being and passing out of being of things. They were also given the powerful instrument—a *permanent* embodiment of words—that endowed them for the first time with a fully ecumenic point of view. Questions hitherto unimaginable were now askable. A new kind of criticism became possible. The mastery that humankind acquired in so depicting itself is there for all to see.

Fatefully, this access of power that unquestionably issued from the reflective isolation and valorization of our explicit, reversible intellectual powers, propagated in this picture of ourselves, was taken as endorsing the ultimacy and comprehensive authority of this representation of humankind in the world in *all* of its modes of being.

The seventeenth century discovery of mathematics as an instrument of research into the natural world not only gave us science and technology, raising to a new magnitude our sense of the power of explicit, reversible intellection; it once and for all immured us in the accompanying partial and parochial picture of humankind in the world.

Within this setting, for me, formed as I am even to the very core of my being by these models and values, to find a new way to think about my situation in the world is the ultimate tour de force. I shall have to conduct my inquiry, at every step remembering that, as indeterminate as it, at any moment, may be, my own mindbody—our jointly present, convivial mindbodies—is the radix upon which the world—our mutual world—is grounded and within the existential matrices of which it will have to be found—indeed, within those very modalities that the regnant view of 2600 years has denegated or obscured. In short, I shall have to return to and endorse myself to my mindbody in the world in which it lives and moves and has its being. For this is the setting in which all entities cohere; the radical matrix of all meaning and meaning discernment, that from which all entities are pretended, that which all entities retrotend, that which in its coition with the world devises figures in which to articulate itself and all that is in some sense or other intractably over against it, it is the condition of the possibility of sentience, motility, and orientation that themselves embody the mute axioms of significance and constitute the primordial ordinations of our being from which articulate speech proceeds.

I sit in my study in the chair in which I customarily do my writing. Those words I have just written and what they bring into being for me—and for you—as well as the words of my commentary upon them and what *they* bring into being for me—and for you—are part of the world, elements of the real. As I was writing these words, as I *now* write *these very* words, there is in the world the background hum of the air conditioner fan—*background* because it endures throughout the time in which I hear the sounds of a passing car and then another and another. There are also the sounds of an English Suite being played on the piano by Glenn Gould. "Piano" does not appear here as the physical object but as the "Piano-note-sound"—not the "harpsichord-note-sound." Glenn

Gould is not the rather frail and stooped man at a keyboard, but the clarity and articulation of Bach's composition, every single note of which I hear at the same time that I "hear," in a different sense, the whole of which they are a part—the whole unmistakably Bach. All these are constituents of the world.

But there is more; of course, infinitely more. My body is a part of it. I both *have* my body and I *am* it. I "have" it because I see my hands before me, one of them grasping a pen. My hands I "have" because they are a kind of part of the visible world as, in a different but analogous sense, the pen I hold is a part of the visible world.

I also *am* my body because it is unique for me among the things before my gaze and I am aware of it kinesthetically and proprioceptively. It is in contact with something that offers it resistance (if we were to talk in abstractions, I might call this the *natural world* or reality), sharply at my left heel resting on the ottoman, dully along the length of my legs, one resting over the other, slightly uncomfortable behind the right knee, not because it impinges upon what I *could* call the natural would, but because of the tension that is there, about half the distance between my heel on ottoman and my writing hand. All this is part of the world. So also is the pressure upon my left buttock, the arthritic pinch in my lower back.

Also in the world before my eyes is the equestrian statue of Alexander the Great and of the Diogenes International Gallery in Plaka of Athens where we first met as night came on; the bronze *Nike* constructed by my friend Evangelos Moustakas on hearing of Bobby Kennedy's assasination. All this is reality, a part of the world.

As I look through the window I see the hanging basket in the patio in which this spring a pair of Carolina wrens built a nest, bringing the grass and fragments of leaves, as Pat and I watched, caught up in the wonder of the works of these small architects, participants in what we could not fail to feel were their hopes, grieving as every single hatchling fell to death in attempting to fly. These all are lineaments of the world.

And the appearance in the world in my words of the small birds and their large hopes brought to ruin, fills the world for some moments with sadness at the death of young birds before their first flight and the death of young children and the death of old men.

Some of these elements of the world are more substantial than others, less evanescent. As difficult to concede as it is for us who have been taught to prize the static and perduring, we are bound to say that every single one of these elements is as real as anything can be when apprehended in the world in which we live and move and have our being; and this is the radical and therefore the privileged point of view. It is certainly the point of view from which I am just now writing these very words.

7/25/90

I step onto the asphalt road, clothed and shod for jogging. On the first ten strides or so the intractable surface on which I run is the rather indeterminate, dull ache in my aging knees, which soon is gone; it is the heaviness of fatigue I feel. It is the end of the jogging week.

The course I run is before me. The first hill I have to climb, beyond the top of which I cannot see, is already in my legs and back and lungs as the effort that the climb will take. The course beyond the hilltop that is out of sight is here just now in the relief I feel in lungs and calves as I descend the far side of the hill that is still out of sight. The difference between the hill that is the anticipation of its effortful climb and that which is the expectation of relief on its far side—both the anticipation and the expectation *presently* embodied, as an effort and the relaxation of that effort—is a function of the dynamic shifting of the focus of my mindbody, which now is invaded, as I glimpse the early morning eastern sky, by "rosy fingered dawn," reflected upon the "wine dark sea," seen from the deck of a ferry leaving Ithaca—and Telemachus and Penelope—as the sun arose.

The several elements that make up the world that my words have made appear are very different. Yet they are all as real as anything can be. They all cohere as a world in my lively mindbody, moving centrifugally, then centripetally, finding its mobile focus first here, then there. I both *have* and am *in the midst of* the world. Living mindbodily is both to be *alternately* moving back and forth between being *in the midst of* the world and *having* the world and *simultaneously being in its midst* and *having* the world.

The world is composed of beliefs, expectations, habits, wonted gestures, the styles and pace of movements, and so on.

Our beliefs about the nature of things about us are seldom the subject of reflection, although of many I can give a report, if asked or if I ask myself. I believe in God, the Father Almighty, maker of heaven and earth; I do not believe in dialectical materialism; I do not believe in capital punishment.

It would be difficult to persuade me to abandon these views. I not only subscribe to the propositions in which they are stated; they have for a very long time underlain not only a host of others of my beliefs, they have been the basis of what I *do,* of what I *have* done, of what I am *given* to doing; they have been sedimented into my mindbody. However, difficult as it would be to persuade me to abandon these beliefs, it is not inconceivable that I might be persuaded.

But what of my "belief" in the principle of induction? I could not formulate this "belief" at the time that I "relied" upon it in order to take my first steps—thereby bringing into being for me a new feature of the world, but more than this: a new *world,* a world that can be seen from an upright posture, a world in which I am motile amidst a new world of objects.

My expectations are seldom given articulate form. I can and do say what they are when asked. Sometimes I am quite surprised by what I have identified as an expectation. Yet it had been there, beneath, perhaps *far* beneath, the level of reflective life. It may be that some inexplicable mood of sadness that welled up in me was due to the disappointment of this "mute" expectation.

Habits are bearers of the real no less than beliefs and expectations. Some of these make an appearance in my awareness, though they need not be less imperious on that account. Some I will discover only in my awkwardness in a novel situation not congenial to what I am given to doing.

If my style of speech is animated and highly gestural, I shall at once *have* and be *in the midst* of the world brought into being by this style of speech. It would all be very different, if I were phlegmatic, laconic, and highly self-contained.

When we speak, quite unselfconciously, of the *world* of medieval serfs, of midwestern American farmers, moving across huge expanses in their combines, of denizens of an urban ghetto, we refer to the beliefs, expectations, habits, wonted gestures, and the styles and pace of their movements that they both *have* and are *in the midst of.*

This is what the real world is: shot through with dynamism, with incessant change, with order, predictability, and coherence, in no wise subject to my whim.

7/26/90

But, you ask, "What has become of the physicist's particle, the biologist's cell, and DNA molecule, the astronomer's quasar?" They are exactly what and where the communities of physicists, biologists, and astronomers say they are.

The history of these—and other natural sciences, though emphatically not those spurious imitators of these—is the history of the devising of figures by these scientists from their mutual mindbodily coition with the world that made these entities present to them, within the history of their activity of investigation. Quarks, DNA molecules, quasars made their appearance in the world and have their standing there as the termini of particular programs of investigation—as substantial as anything can be; but having made their appearance there only through the convivial mindbodily doings and sayings of scientist, with their instruments of research—conceptual and material. For these substantial entities to exist in the world is for them to reside in the history and present practice of the convivial mindbodily transactions with them of the men and women who are their discoverers. This is the truth—though it is partial—in the instrumentalist theory of science. The world of the sciences is the outcome of the means and modes of their investigations.

So, they exist only in the mind? Emphatically not. They exist in the world and the world appears in the articulations of our convivial, mutually copresent mindbodies; and this world we both *have* and are *in the midst of*—mindbodily.

By now it should be clear that the world is not a determinate and static set of entities that exists in itself, independent of its appearance within human apprehensions, opposed to which are the fugitive beliefs, expectations, habits, wonted gestures, the style and pace of our movements, the "mere" contents of our consciousness—the dualism, however formulated according to current philosophic fashion, of extended things over against thinking, insubstantial, fluctuant, and inconstant things.

This Cartesian dualism has been repeatedly subjected to philosophic trashings. Yet nothing changes; it only grows worse. The Academy and now increasingly the literate general culture are quite mad from it—even those within it who would be its critics.

Yet we have only to surrender the curious notion, born of the philosophic tradition, that the world as we perfectly well know it to be in our quotidian doings and sayings is on the contrary something the existence of which can *be known independent of our knowledge of it,* something that exists apart from our embodiment in it.

We of course cannot "surrender this curious notion" because it is no notion. Or put another way, even though we can be brought by" intellectual "persuasion to withhold our notional assent, our real assent is so deeply embedded in the beliefs, expectations, habits, wonted gestures, and styles of our convivial mindbodies in the world that for us to change would be nothing less than the dismantling of the world itself. Yet, in another sense, it is all so easy. We need only recover and accredit ourselves in the primary world in which we, at this very moment, live and move and have our being.

The acropolis of Mycenae that appears in the world as I sit in my study writing these words is a hill that emerges from the plain of Argos, capped by the ruins of the Palace of Agamemnon. It is not in the world as it is for the geologist *insofar as and for as long as* it is the object of his geological interest—however else it is in the world for him under different circumstances for his mindbody.

Nor is it in the world as it is for the team of archaeologists, with their trowels and brushes, under the cruel gaze of the midday sum.

It appears in the world, as I sit here writing, as the site of Agamemnon's murder by Clytemnestra, as the place, perhaps, where the Trojan War was first conceived, where I stood and read aloud to Pat Auden's poem, "The Shield of Achilles"—"Iron-hearted manslaying Achilles / Who would not live long." That place and the great epics of Homer flow into my being as I sit here writing, as it flows into me when I stand upon its windswept summit. No single element of this entity in the world is in the least bit equivocal in comparison with what is in the world for the geologist or the archaeologist. Homer's epics, Auden's poem are fully accredited vectors of the real.

"Neither the language of science nor the language of poetry may be said to enjoy a *context-neutral* privilege as the vector of the nature of things." Now, can we not see that a shadow of the old dualism is still cast over this formulation. There is in it, in the image of a vector, a suggestion that language carries reality, which is "over there," to us who are "over here." Whereas we now know the relation between the world and ourselves to be more radical than that.

The *world,* then, is my mindbody—our convivial mindbodies—viewed from the perspective of what is more or less distal to it, dynamically over against it at the termini of its pretensions—both operative and active; my *mindbody*—our convivial mindbodies—is the world viewed from the perspective of what is proximal to it, focused in it as the concentering of its retrotensions—operative and active.

No. This does not leave us with some strange new kind of idealism—as if the world and my mindbody are both mere free floating and fugitive "contents of consciousness" and no more intractable than such would be.

Being—as insistent, as intractable as can be—is continually asseverating itself as what it is, being taken up by and articulated through my—through our—convivial mindbodily life.

So envisioned, the world is substantial and intractable; but it is not static and determinate—not a world existing in independence of its presence to our jointly copresent selves.

Are not, though, all distinctions effaced in a night in which all cows are black? Not at all. The world is as stable, as rich, as individuated and as complex as we all know it to be, even in the space of a few moments, within the texture of our quotidian life.

All the choirs of heaven and all the furniture of earth are exactly as we have always known and now know them to be.

Only the power of the image of a reader before a page of written, permanent words, together with our sense of mastery over the world provided by chirography, could have seduced us into believing that all *serious* reflection about the nature of things and humankind's place in their midst—as distinct from that in our ordinary sayings and doings—should be governed by these models and these alone. And for 2600 years, because of this, we have become increasingly problematic to ourselves.

7/29/90

It is of course taken for granted that we learn from experience; and *experience* is a word that is indispensable to our second-order talk about the nature of things.

Yet the use of both *experience* and *learn* in this proposition is, without further interpretation, multiply ambiguous. Until these words are appropriated to some specific theater of reflection,[k] with a particular stage setting, their meaning can be any of a very large number of unspecified possibilities.

In our culture of the printed word our even offhanded remark, "We learn from experience," will often import a stage setting for these words such that we imagine experience as like a book and learning from it as like reading.

How, different from this, will *learning from experience* be understood in the alternative stage setting provided implicitly in my argument here?

Experience taken as that which befalls us in the course of life does not come to us raw. Rather it is formed dialectically in the crossing points between our convivial mindbodies and the indeterminate other, made manifest in vectors of their own devising: in their wonted, even

[k]See *A Philosophical Daybook,* pp. 59ff; Appendix, pp. 195–203.

their primitive, movements that explore and express their limits in space and time; in their postural deployment vis-à-vis the indeterminate other, waiting to appear in the world; in their motility and increasingly articulated, discriminating, and more and more richly textured sentience.

That logos that underlies and informs the pretensive-retrotensive activity of our lively mindbodies in the world issues at length in language, properly speaking: in words and their accustomed uses; in short in *usages,* which is to say, in concepts.

Since, then, experience does not come to us raw it can teach us only what we have been taught to learn from it by ourselves and our fellows. What befalls us addresses questions to us that practice has taught us to hear it ask; it interrogates us because antecedently it has been made manifest through our interrogations.

This is to be seen at the most primitive levels of our being and also at the most advanced, articulated, and reflective levels.

For example, only by coordinating the large and fine muscles of their eyes can neonates bring vision, hence visibility, into being for themselves, so that they can then see what appears to sight. At the reflective level, learning the use of the pronouns *I* and *you* makes possible, in the course of life, the discovery and iterated *re*covery of persons and of responsibility, without having learned which usages they—persons and responsibility—could not exist for us.

7/30/90

For an entity or meaning to stand forth within the fabric of our world—in short, to *exist,* to *be*—is for it to have been summoned forth from the matrix of the "indeterminate other" by our multifarious languages—the sum of the figures that our mindbodies have at once devised for themselves out of their own primordial ordinations and found in and appropriated from their cultural mise en scène, that they both *have* and are *in the midst of*.

With the expression *indeterminate other* I mean to refer to the *thisness—hecceity,* as scholastic philosophers called it—that asserts itself from within the *particularity* of every thing that is summoned forth in our modes of discourse, insofar as its sheer unarticulable *thisness* "overflows" and is oppugnant to discourse. I also mean the more ecumenic sense we have that our existence at every moment is environed by, but stands out against an as-yet-unreflected but quite intractable substantiality—a "something I know not what" (to use an idiom of John Locke), Being—that asseverates itself through everything that appears. Our overdetermined languages with their polyvalent surpluses of meaning call forth and arrest the world of things. The logics of these languages—those implicated in our movement, sentience, orientation; the languages of gesture, gait, speech-rhythm; of common sense, poetry, "empirical" description, scientific explanation, axiology, eschatology—appear incommensurable with one another viewed from a detached point of view. In fact, however, they cohere in our convivial acts of speaking and appropriating speech, since *in* these acts they jointly retrotend the very mindbodies wherein are rooted the figures in which our world is formed.

However useful—indeed, necessary—may be a *conceptual* distinction between an entity and the complex and historically dense web of signs, gestures, and meanings that bring it forth and sustain it, no fundamental *ontological* space exists between a thing and the vectors that bear it forth, save only its mute and opposing *thisness.* A thing's actuality, its concreteness overflowing language, is identical with its appearance within the textures of what we say and write.

We came to suppose otherwise only when the paradigm of the relation between our languages on one side—as we came to think of them—and the world on the other began to be drawn from images of a print culture; that is, when words came to be alienated in our reflection from their *use* by actual speakers and hearers in our oral-aural life where no distinction exists between the *world* in which we live and move and have our being and *the asseverations that bring it forth.*

If I hold up a rectangular object and say, "This is the ace of trumps," I will have summoned forth from the indeterminate other a more determinate entity than I will have, if I say of the rectangular object," This is the ace of spades." A fortiori, both of these will be more determinate than the entity that I summon forth with the words, "This is a playing card."

The *nature* of the "ace of trumps," "the ace of spades," and "a playing card" is, in each case, identical with the actuality that each has in the discourse that summons it forth.

One can of course "reduce" the "ace of trumps" to "the ace of spades" and the latter to "a playing card" by assigning a logical (and therefore an ontological) privilege to the discourse that embodies the less determinate entity, just as one can further reduce a "cardlike physical object" to "a particular organization of atoms" simply by according a privilege to the discourse of physics for summoning forth this erstwhile "playing card" from the matrix of the indeterminate other.

Now obviously we move with great ease and without taking notice from one of these forms of discourse to another, according to the interest at hand and to the actuality that a given discourse has summoned forth. Ontological bedrock however is reached in every one of these discourse modes. The actuality of the "ace of trumps" in the game, contract bridge, is no less ontologically substantial and underived than "cardlike physical object" or "a particular arrangement of atoms" *just because the discourse that summons it forth is the product of a contract,* negotiated within a game—as we might be tempted to suppose. The ground of *all* forms of discourse and the actualities that they summon forth is the contracts that we have negotiated—explicitly, as with the game contract bridge; but only tacitly "negotiated" (or not *negotiated* at all) in the overwhelming majority of other cases—and these we routinely endorse in our every authentic act of speech, whatever the discourse we use.

8/6/90

Earlier I said that romanticism laid claim to "imagination" as a countervailing reality to the Enlightenment's regnant intellectualism, but in such a way as to overlook the continuity between our so-called creative powers and the exercise of instrumental reason.

Two matters here require amplification: What are the grounds upon which I base a claim to continuity, what disanalogies nevertheless underlie the supposition of distinct powers that can be called *imagination,* as over against explicit intellection?

Piaget has made, in a quite different connection, a distinction that is useful here; that, namely, between reversible and irreversible intelligence. Reversible intelligence is exhibited in feats of intellection that proceed on the basis of premises that have been or, in any case, could be explicitly identified as such; irreversible intelligence proceeds toward a novel, hitherto undisclosed coherence or meaning upon "premises" that have not and could not be identified as such.

In writing the preceding sentences, for example, I relied upon the *grammatical* premises implicated with my native language on my way toward articulating a grammatical sentence in English, even though I did not have to attend explicitly to the grammatical rules—or only when I found myself in some doubt; nor was the telos of achieving an intelligible sentence ever *explicitly* before me. Insofar as we analyze what I just did in *this* way we will see the feat of writing as the exercise, albeit largely tacit, of *reversible* intelligence.

Analyzed differently, that is to say, singling out for attention a different stratum of the event of my writing, there is disclosed in these self-same sentences a feat of *irreversible* intelligence. Using the English language as an instrument of research, I embodied a novel and hitherto undisclosed because as yet indeterminate coherence and meaning—that is, *what I wanted to say*—that could not be made explicit before the fact of its embodiment in my words; and this is no less true, even if I have said the very same thing before. *As I began to write,* my relation to what I *thought* was that to an as yet unarticulated, novel meaning—a thought that issues from a nisus toward the realization of coherence that, though as yet mute, is already inarticulately portended in the logos of my mindbody.

It is the *disanalogies* between the exercise, on the one hand, of these powers of reversible intelligence and, on the other, of those of irreversible intellection that lend support to the view that our intellectual powers can manifest themselves in different forms of specialization and that therefore it is legitimate to *contrast* "imagination" with instrumental reason.

We must not however overlook the *analogies* between reversible and irreversible intelligence—which, I have suggested, the romantic reaction to the "intellectuality" of the Enlightenment has tended to do. In doing this it conceded too much, weakened its case and impoverished our conception of both reversible and irreversible reason.

8/7/90

As real as are these disanalogies, however, it may well be that even our *routine* exercise of our intellectual powers is irreducibly interpenetrated by an irreversible, "creative" element.

In the case of my writing a clear, grammatical sentence in English, in the preceding illustration, I may be said to have followed the rules of grammar and syntax, however unreflected those rules may have been in course. By tacitly *inferring* in accordance with rules tacitly recognized, I was led to place the words of the emerging sentence in their syntactically correct position relative to one another; led, too, to establish agreement among them as to tense, mood, number, person, and so forth. This procedure is *explicit* inference, that is, reversible reasoning, not because the premises and rules of inference are in the instant case *explicit,* for they are not, but because, if need be, they can be rendered so: I can move from the conclusion (the grammatically correct sentence) to the premises (explicitable rules of grammar and syntax); hence, reversible reasoning.

If we look more closely however we will see that the exercise of *reversible* reasoning is in fact dependent upon *irreversible* reasoning—as difficult as this is to notice because of an established habit of ours of overlooking it.

The condition of the possibility of my drawing from the premises implicit in grammar and syntax the inferences according to the rules of inference, also implicit there, is the performance of feats of *judgment.* I have to judge that the word toward which I have been groping is the one that will contribute to the *clear* saying of what I wish to say, I have to judge its appositeness in the context of the other words in the emerging sentence and, most important, *I have to judge that I am correctly applying the rules of grammar and syntax to the particular words that are here in use.* This act of judging is itself an irreversible procedure. I cannot give explicit rules by which I arrived at the judgments, just as I cannot give a rule for applying a rule to a particular case, a rule for using a word to single out a particular. Writing and speaking about the world, even in our most ordinary doings and sayings, is shot through with and utterly dependent upon these irreversible acts of judgment, everyone of them "creative." Yet—as you would expect me to say—they are not "irrational," for they depend upon the logos, the mute axioms of significance that are implicated with our primordial mindbodily sentience, motility and orientation in the world.

In reading I come upon the word *Infundibulum.* Nothing in the context offers a clue as to its use (how by the way, would a context offer such clue? not surely by "hinting" at an explicit rule of inference); although the "fun" in the word suggests (*how* does it "suggest?" how do I *take* the suggestion?) something having to do with a funnel—do not ask me why.

I turn to the dictionary. There I read: *"Infundibulum,"* n. pl.—la. *Anat.* 1. A funnel shaped organ or part. 2. A funnel shaped extension of the hypothalamus connecting the pituitary gland to the base of the brain. 3. A space in the right ventricle at the base of the pulmonary artery."[1]

I know immediately that the word is being used as a metaphor; I know immediately that its context does not deal with anatomy. How do I know this? By an act of irreversible, that is, "creative" judgment.

But how does the metaphor do its work? I try to imagine various analogies between *infundibulum* as metaphor and each of the three possible meanings given for it in the dictionary. To discover the way in which the word does its metaphorical work, I have irreversibly to judge that meaning given by the dictionary that is most analogous with what might be its sense in the text I am reading. I also of course must discern at the same time that dictionary meaning that is least *disanalogous* with the use of *infundibulum* in its context in what I am reading. How do I do this? Only by irreversible acts of judgment—all carried out with greater ease and speed than any act of explicit, reversible inference drawing from explicit premises would be.

Even though there are, then, these disanalogies between reversible and irreversible intelligence, leading us to posit the existence of a separate, "creative" faculty, it is clear that reversible reasoning, which romanticism imputed to scientific inquiry and at times made into a kind of bug-a-boo, would be quite impotent without irreversible imagination; that all reasoning is at bottom—from which all forms of reasoning derive—*imagining.*

---

[1]*American Heritage Dictionary.*

All our rational powers, however formalized they may be, as with mathematics and logic; however specialized they may become for the purpose of devising theories of the natural world, writing a sonnet, painting the ceiling of the Sistine Chapel, composing—*or performing*—Bach's *Suites for Unaccompanied Cello,* or beholding and interpreting all these, or even comprehending the words that you have just read, derive from the creative because at bottom irreversible powers of our mindbodies. For these do not at their radix live by drawing formal inferences from explicit premises according to rules, but rather by surrendering to their own heuristic demands for meaning, value, and coherence in the world.

Imagination, then, is our mindbodily life as sentient, motile, and oriented, viewed in the light of our performance of these irreversible feats.

Romanticism was prepared to be content, if need be, with the half-a-loaf that would be supplied by imagination as an essentially separate and countervailing reality to the putatively harsh demands of reversible intelligence.

By means of the preceding analysis, "hard" intellectuality and "soft" imagination are restored to their true relation; and into the bargain we gain a better conception of the place of humankind in the nature of things.

(I find this analysis most unsatisfying, for in its attempt to single out various features of the transactions involved, it, inescapably of course, suggests that these features are somehow rather precariously connected. All of the natural rhythms of intellection, reversible and ireversible, have disappeared in the analysis. In fact of course writing, speaking, or interpreting a sentence is as easy and as unreflected as walking across your own living room cold sober.)

8/8/90

For all of this being self-evident once you have penetrated the veil obtruded between us and these rudimentary facts by the second-order account of human intellection, born in our literacy and borne by our philosophical tradition, the old dualism persists.

I read these words:[m] "Imagination alone can never conjure up the sensation of mountains, you need the aching thighs, the thinning air, the stones under your feet." An utterly harmless remark taken as no more than the incontrovertible claim that there is an important difference between actually clambering up the unforgiving, rocky slopes of the mountains of Crete and a secondhand report on doing so. Yet our well-known dualism underlies this off-hand remark. Imagination, conceived as a "mental" something or other, cannot conjure up *anything* since, discarnate, it would lack the wherewithal for conjuring. Indeed, it is only because my imagination is *not* alone, because the "aching thighs" of my own mountain climbing—or even of just my vigorous walking after an illness—are, *as I read,* mindbodily present that I can understand the meaning of the distinction that Powell wishes to draw. And had not the "aching thighs, the thinning air, the stones under [her] feet" not been contemporaneously present to *her* mindbody-as-imagination while she was actually writing down these words, she could not have apprehended the distinction between climbing up the side of Mt. Ida and writing a report on doing so. Climbing and imagining a climb are certainly two different things. Yet even an imaginary climb is a

[m]Dilys Powell, *The Villa of Ariadne.*

climb—aching thighs, thinning air, stones under your feet, and all the rest.

Imagination has its being at the chiasma between my mindbody, whether narrowly or broadly construed, and the world, whether at a given moment its focus is sharp of soft.

My friend Moustakas, the Greek sculptor, says to me: "Come. I want to make a sculpture for your birthday; but you must come into the studio and watch me do it." And so we go.

I have no idea what this is to be. It is immediately clear to me from watching the gross deployment of his body, the tilt of his head as he moves, the cast of his eyes, the rhythms of his movements, the way he hefts his hammer, the way he holds and positions and shifts about a bronze sheet 12 × 18 inches and a sixteenth of an inch thick that what will eventually achieve embodiment in an object in the world that will be between and over against us both is already moving through his mindbody toward a consummation. At this stage, the sculpture has its sole existence as the telos of his mindbodily intentions. There has been no preliminary sketch—about the making of which, had there been one, the same kind of analysis would have to be made as with the procedures in which he is now engaged.

He holds the sheet of bronze before his studying gaze, turns it this way and that, sights along its edge, first lengthwise and then along its width. I have the powerful sense that the sculpture that is to be is already proleptically in his hands, at the tips of his fingers, that imagination—which is to say, his whole mindbodily being—has come to a focus at the point where his hands and the sheet of bronze meet. Imagination thus dwells in such ordinary things of the world.

He takes a pair of heavy shears and makes a cut into the sheet of bronze. The sculpture that is to be begins to move for the first time from its dwelling in the privacy of his mindbody (this is not true; it moves from one form of public existence to another, differently realized one) into the world in which we are jointly present and present to one another. Imagination is now in the muscular pressure of his hands upon the handles of the shears as they shape the very particular curve that he is cutting into the bronze. In this cutting and in this cut are drawn out of his mindbody the sculpture that until this moment was only and entirely there, but now begins to make its appearance between us. Imagination is equally in the motif of the act of *shaping* and in the realizing *shape.*

Now grasping the sheet of bronze in his leather-gloved left hand along its lengthwise side and resting the opposing edge at an angle on his wooden bench, he begins to strike the sheet with a heavy hammer, along an axis that runs parallel to its two long sides; and just as the hammer strikes he imparts a torque to its head to stretch the sheet into a concavity. Imagination is in the arm and hand that delivers the torque, because the concavity taking shape in the bronze to form the sculpture is *already* in the form of the force of the arm and hand that shapes to this particular telos; it is also in the gaze that monitors and coordinates the hammer's blows with the emerging shaping.

By now the two long sides can be brought together and welded to form a hollow bronze tube. Suddenly that gestalt which struggled to take shape from the movements and rhythms of his mindbody, now sweatingly at work, appears before me for the first time as what it will be—a bird. Imagination is in my mindbodily act of apprehending the bird that is portended in the brazen "tube."

In due course the sculpture is finished—*Bird in Flight*—and mounted on its marble base, and solemnly presented to me with appropriate praises of my longevity.

Later, as we sipped ouzo in his apartment and talked of making sculptures, Moustakas shockingly drew me up short by pointing to his head and saying: "The imagination is here."

Recovering my composure, I replied: "And why is it not here? (pointing to my lips) Why is it not here? (pointing to my finger-tips) Why is it not here? (pointing to my chest) Why is it not here? (making a slashing movement through the air with my arm)."

As I said and did these things a shock of recognition appeared in his eyes; and with the passion characteristic of the Greeks, preeminently of Moustakas, he arose from his chair, came toward me with tears in his eyes, embraced me and said: "Beel, this is the truth."

8/14/90

It seems to be a deeply entrenched habit with me to depict reflection as quite discontinuous with the as yet unreflected. Yet how could this have any serious philosophic import?

Sitting in the solitude of my study, engaged in no practical activity save only that of writing down these *reflected* words about the phenomenon of reflection, nothing opposes me except the already written words above the point at which the tip of my pen flows along the printed blue line of the notebook's page and the blank expanse beneath that point and partly obscured by the hand that holds the pen. Not even another person is present. All is silence.

The pace at which the words appear on the page is subject solely to my control. The *significant* elements of what is going on here, are my focused acts of reflection, my search for the apposite and accurate word, my acts of writing; all else is subordinate or nonexistent—the many interruptions of my train of thought, the ringing of the telephone, my woolgathering gaze out the window, my struggle to capture a fugitive image as I—why?—intently study the face of Lorenzo Il Magnifico, hanging on my wall.

A frame is placed around the content of these occurrences by the lucid, focused reflection upon the nature of reflection that can appear in this theater. What appears here is a lucid, centered awareness opposed to its objects that are clearly "out in front of me" as the words I write are "out in front of me," but as the words I *speak* are not.

There is no sense here of the forward surge of time as there always is in the oral-aural reciprocity. On the contrary, all "occurs" here as in a kind of "eternity." The invasions from the world of time—the woolgathering gaze out the window, the interruptions of my train of thought—have all been bracketed out by the frame imposed by the picture of focused ratiocination, removed as far as possible from the hurly-burly of lively speech. And what is bracketed out is not real, is without significance, in any case, no part of the feat of reflection. Reflection is just what we see here.

I cannot imagine a preliterate man reflecting in *any* way upon reflection; even less reflecting in *this* way. The description that I have written earlier is clearly the work of one who has introjected the images and values of the world of print.

But look at what has been excluded as having no value, no real part in a feat of reflection: all those acts and behaviors of my mindbody in the world that identify it as existing in a particular time and place. The frame placed around the content of these occurrences—lucid acts of detached reflection, understood as *articulation in written word*—has eliminated these. Not only is the pneumocarnal embodiment of reflection obscured; the contribution of these disvalued behaviors to the realization of reflection is denigrated. Most important of all, the logical range of words like *reflection, rational, logos,* and so on is defined by the regnancy among denizens of a print culture of *this* depiction of reflection. But let us challenge this.

I am, in solitude, engaged in a common form of practical activity for a householder: repairing a broken electrical switch. In silence, I study the replacement switch. New technology has produced a switch different from any I have ever installed. But the logic of one electrical switch is really identical with every other. I hold it in my hand and study it. I study the wiring in the wall from which the broken fixture has been disconnected. Anyone observing me doing this would recognize that I am *studying* all this with a practical end in view—not admiring the aesthetics of the design of the new switch. Although I could readily say what I was "concluding" about all this, were I asked, in no sense am I, in the absence of the question, "concluding" anything about it, "to myself," in words. If we, for discussion, isolate a certain intentional tract of my mindbodily being, letting the discovery of the broken fixture be the *terminus a quo* and the completed installation of the new one the *terminus ad quem,* we can readily imagine that all the while that I am moving between these termini I am silently and nonverbally "concluding" all sorts of connections, even though, if asked—let us say, by the clerk in the hardware store—I could say what I was looking for and why, and so forth.

During the whole course of this process I have been subject only to my own pace, and even if I meet a friend en route, I will not forget, my whole mindbody will continue to be oriented toward the goal of my activity. I have been exempt from the forward surge of time that the presence of other human interlocutors and respondents, to whom I am responsible in the oral-aural reciprocity, imposes. Yet—and there is nothing either remarkable or controversial in the claim—there is throughout the course of this intentional tract what we can now call *reflection in course,* to contrast it with the *detached reflection* of the first case. And if I feel uncomfortable with such a claim, as I do, it is because *detached reflection* is for me paradigmatic of reflection as such.

There is of course another form of *reflection in course,* that, namely, which pervades our oral-aural exchanges. It is not only that I perform an exegesis of every word you say—instantaneously and without difficulty; I do this not at my own pace but subject to the forward surge of time introduced by *your* presence and *your* rhythm. Furthermore even as I am already moving forward in my act of speech, I *monitor* what I am already in the process of saying. There are things I wish not to say; there are things I wish *not* to be *taken* as saying; there are better and more apposite ways of saying what I wish to say; yet the *better* way, clearer, more persuasive, is not the translation of an inept English sentence into a felicitous one. My words are monitored—they do not just rush forth unsuperintended; they are monitored by reflection in course.

Now, nothing is either surprising or controversial

about this. It is something that we are well acquainted with since we put it into practice all day long. It is worth saying at all only because our captivity to the paradigm of detached reflection that is the creature of our literacy, causes us to overlook or disvalue the logos that pervades the whole of our mindbodily life in all the forms of our reflection in course.

8/15/90

In the course of my argument against Derrida and de Man I declare rather emphatically that no *ontological* dualism between an eternal realm and the temporal world in which I live and move and have my being is tenable, conceding of course that a *conceptual distinction* between them is possible, often necessary.

Reading this over, I find myself wondering precisely what this claim amounts to and how I could hold such a view and at the same time believe in the *existential* reality of the *ontological,* as opposed to the mere conceptual, actuality of transcendence.

The mindbodily actuality of myself that I apprehend by means of reflection in course as I am engaged in the activity of jogging or repairing a broken light switch, or in that of a dialectical exchange with other participants in an oral-aural colloquy, is one that is continually establishing its connection with the immediate world of time and sense. Sometimes in rather dramatic ways this mindbody becomes aware of itself as it meets the intractable limits of the world.

By contrast, the mindbodily actuality of myself that I apprehend by means of reflection in course as I am engaged in mathematical heuristics, even if I may be brought back to my concrete actuality by the pressure against the intractable limits of the world at the end of the pen with which I write out the tokens that I use, is as attenuated as anything can be.

The contrast between my apprehended mindbody in the one case and in the other is so great that the temptation is well-nigh irresistible to believe that, whereas in the first case I am immured by the bonds and ligatures of the mundane world of time and history, in the second I have slipped these bonds and become a discarnate extramundane intellect dwelling among eternal relations in an eternity.

Some such contrast was perceived in that between the fleeting hurly-burly of oral-aural existence and the majestic stasis and "eternity" of the written word. And as we know, it was out of the new technology of chirography and its transvaluation of values that our philosophical tradition arose and in the imperialism of its hegemony placed a veil between our thought and our quotidian actuality.

It is out of an experience of such a contrast as this that time comes to be opposed to eternity, becoming to being, the mundane world to an eternal realm, *dóxa* to *epistéme.* Less than a moment's reflection reveals of course that these are but contrasting *modes* in which my mindbody dwells in the only world there is; and that 'time' is a concept I have derived from my dwelling in one of these modes and 'eternity' is a concept derived from my dwelling in the other. It is the same mindbody that dwells first in one mode of its being in the world and then in another mode.

There is therefore—if we wish to put it so—an *actual* difference between one of these ways and another for my mindbody to dwell in the only world there is.

Therefore, though we use the concepts 'time' and

'eternity' to refer, respectively, to these two modes, their differences are *not* merely conceptual but *actual.* Yet their actuality is that of different modes of *my* actual mindbodily being in the one and only world that *is* actual.

8/16/90

Can, then, anything radically *discontinuous* assert itself in the midst of my mindbodily life—that is here so far depicted as *continuous* through and through, from top to bottom, from abstract to concrete? Can any *novelty* arise within the context of the *uniform,* any actuality that, even though dependent upon its worldly ground, is ontologically irreducible to the setting from which it issues forth? Can anything be said to transcend the world as it has here been rendered?

The answer is, of course, Yes. Such an actuality appears, such a novelty asserts itself, such a transcending of my worldly ground occurs every single time that I speak in my own name, every time that I accept responsibility for the world as mine that I have received from the hand of God.

In speaking, I of course depend upon my biological past and that of the race, upon the history of our native language and its etymology, on its grammar, syntax, and semantical resources, on the usages of my particular speech-community, and so on.

The *act* whereby I speak—not merely sound—my words as my own and am prepared, as we say, to stand by them, to own them, to be willing to be taken at them is just such an actuality, just such a novelty, just such a discontinuity, just such a transcending. And this is the case every single time that I speak, no matter how routine and unremarkable may be the occasion and sense of my words.

The act in which I bring forth a novelty in every authentic speaking is the paradigm of action as such; as owning and standing by my words is the paradigm of the human-making act of taking responsibility. My freedom—no mere moral certainty, but an omnipresent *actuality,* the very paradigm, if you please, of the "stubborn irreducible *fact*"—is not that, since in speaking I transcend *from* the world, I am thereby disentrammeled of its "causalities," for I am not, even if I may be said to bring forth a new reality. It is rather the power I have for taking responsibility.

8/20/90

I am standing in a shopping mall and am for a moment seized by a mild and fugitive attack of amnesia. This is not the familiar case of ordinary absentmindedness: "Let me see, what did I come in here to do?" I do not have to consult the driver's licence that is in my wallet to be able to give my name and current address.

What I experience is a deeper sense of estrangement from myself and from the world—for the brief moment that it lasts, more disturbing than a familiar instance of forgetfulness. For just a breath there is an existential queasiness in the pit of my stomach.

But for this last, I might feel that this sense of disaffection that I feel is a mark of my transcendence of the given world, my unassimilability to its regularities, my freedom as spirit. But this is different; and it is not exhilarating.

I glance about, looking for some clue of why this

place is *this* place rather than some other. There is none. Indeed, this is not even a *place.*

For to be a *place* it would have to present some unique overture to this concrescent density that is indeterminately and dynamically at the center of the world, namely, my own lively, sentient, motile and oriented mindbody. There is nothing of this sort in this mall for this moment. With this paradigm *place* in the world that is my mindbodily being there is nothing here that is uniquely commensurate.

Every single specialty shop I see as I glance about is one of a national chain of such shops. This mall, so perceived, is one of a theoretically infinite number of identical malls. There is no mark of this mall being *this* one rather than *that.* There are no shops that are recognizably local businesses with a history of service to and affiliation with this—or *any*—particular community. Nothing here speaks uniquely of or to the history of *my* forty-five years of life in these environs. This mall is not for me an environs. There is no place here for me because there is nothing uniquely commensurate with my past, my future, my present mindbodily being, apart from our mere physical juxtaposition. Perhaps this is what Gertrude Stein meant when, years ago, she said of Oakland, California: "There is no *there* there."

For the brief duration of my fugitive mood, struck by the radical substitutability of this mall, by its, in this sense, utter abstractness, *I* for an instant become an abstraction, no longer myself the paradigm place from which all my efferent pretensions arise, to which all my afferent retrotensions refer. I am become a spatial entity in infinite space; I have been displaced: *De*placed, really.

This sense of deplacement is a familiar one for modern man, as Pascal was the first to suggest: ". . . I am frightened, and astonished at being here rather than there: for there is no reason why here rather than there, why now rather than then . . ."

It is within my paradigmatic mindbodily place—whether at a given moment its range is extensive or narrow—that I feel at home because it contains the objects and relations upon which I have left my personal stamp, expressed my idiosyncrasy, part of my unique history; it is the place where all the goals I seek, all the objects of my personal fulfillment, all the ends of my personal moral action are. It is the place where all my griefs have their habitation.

My place however is not only these. It is a whereon to stand, it is status, it is room. Drawn away from these concrete bonds to the concrete, my being is contracted into an abstract entity that is no*where* in particular at no particular *time.*

When therefore poststructuralist literary theory appears to propose the displacement of the authoritative voice of the text, the self of the reader, and to declare the meaning of signs to be ultimately undecidable, this is best interpreted not as the enunciation of a new critical norm, but the acquiescence in a fait accompli. The alienation that was intensified in the Cartesian program issues in the capitulation of the thinking thing to an objective realm of extended things that exist and can be "known," even in the absence of any knower, ends with its consummation in the *humanus abscondatus:* the writer has disappeared; the reader has disappeared; even the critic who tells us this, and its telling, have disappeared.

The terrible irony that all this is in fact quite impossible is kept in obscurity by our steadfast refusal to abandon our second-order account of things, in which we do not live, since it is impossible so to do, in favor of recovering the radical mindbodily being that each one of us is, that all of us together are, in the world in which we live and move and have our being in our ordinary sayings and doings.

8/21/90

A professional actress friend tells me that when she forgets her lines on stage she recovers herself by repeating the "business," in which she is usually engaged when she speaks the lines that have gotten away—lighting a cigarette, serving a martini, tossing her head and combing her hair with her fingers.

As the lines when spoken without incident do not flow from her mind, so they are not to be recovered when lost by "cudgelling the brain".

Learning the part preparatory to an opening night is not the repeated reading of her lines from a script in order that they may be drilled into her *mind.* It is rather a sustained act of disposing her ductile mindbody to incorporate the role. At a certain point she will have to read her lines aloud—even in solitude. Why? If she is to be the character she is to play, she will have to begin to appear in the world as this character, to body it forth, accompanying her sounded words with the postures and the gestures that begin to flow spontaneously from her mindbodily being as, in reading, she more and more incarnates in the world through herself in the world the person that she is to play.

Very soon she will have to "play" the part with another member of the cast so that the "lines" of each—very quickly they will cease to be *lines* and will become *what each says* as the character that he and she are—may alternate contrapuntally, thoroughly ensconced amidst the balletic movements of their bodies and gestures, appearing more and more fully incarnate in a world that has been brought into being in these very words and movements, that in turn more and more fully evoke the gestures and intonations demanded by that world.

To memorize a part is, in stages, to come mindbodily to dwell in a world, in the company of others, that has its being through these very acts. Momentarily to "forget" one's lines is, for a moment, to absent oneself from that world. To *remember* is to take up that world again, grasping that part of it that lies most ready to hand.

Memory is not something, then, that is husbanded by the mind—as we are in this tradition inclined to suppose. It is inextricably implicated with the usages and artifacts of our convivial mindbodily life in the midst of the cultural and natural world—even in the repertoire of our motor skills.

Only the tacit Cartesianism of this culture reiterates to us a contrary view, over and over. In our quotidian life we know the truth and routinely act upon it. When I misplace my specs, I reenact my life and movements during the time before they "disappeared," grasping a part of the world in which this disappearance occurred that comes most readily to hand.

Nor is this dependence of memory, without which I would cease to be human, upon the relative permanence of those unique points of contact between the world and this density that is the center of the world for me a matter of merely academic interest. In a culture in which "all that is solid melts into air," memory is in grave jeopardy.

I lie on my bed to take an afternoon nap. Gradually, irresistibly I am seized by the sharp—I was about to say "recollection" but it is something else, a *presently actual reenactment* of my being born. I am neither awake nor asleep. This is neither wakeful reality nor a dream world. I am in a state to which none of these terms applies.

It is my body, neither the body of wakeful reality nor that of a dream, that moves slowly and painfully through excruciating narrowness—*angustiae*—so I say after the fact, as I try to reenact in words this reenactment. The terror that is now upon me is not that of the reflective being that I now am. It is the primitive, animal terror of an unborn infant being born; a terror that is experienced *as terror* in the as-yet-unreflecting body. It is the dread encounter with *angustiae,* the narrowness and pain of the birth canal for a being that has known until now the tranquility and security of the womb and is now coming to know—and not knowing in any reflective way, but profoundly *knowing* nonetheless—a new reality that is a betrayal of all the promises that uterine life had made.

When at last I am born I am overwhelmed by a grief such as I have never known, at a loss for which there is no consolation, and at promises of never failing succor that cannot be fulfilled, promises that were tendered by my mother's womb to my embryonic mindbody.

And then I wept, shoulder-heavingly, for hours.

This "event" in my prehistory is an event in my history only as its antecessor, until I discover, name and claim it as my own. This too is memory, as far as it could be from the Cartesian *Cogito.*

As these two cases make plain, memory is husbanded in all the modalities of my mindbodily existence, ranging from the highly abstract fantasy of an equation written on a slip of paper—a fantasy, let us not forget, that itself derives from because it is incarnate in my mindbody—to the tightly concrete promises received by and remembered, even to this very moment, in the tissues of my embryonic mindbody. Memory, as does imagination, has its being at the chiasma between my mindbody, whether narrowly or broadly construed, and the world, whether at a given moment its focus is sharp or soft.

Now, of course, we all know this quite well; even to remark it is rather embarrassing. When however we decide in this culture to give the matter some "serious thought," memory migrates to the mind, (as opposed to the body) in due course finding its way, if we elect to be *truly* serious, to the engrams of the brain.

8/22/90

I have earlier shown that scientific, that is to say, putatively exhaustively reversible, reasoning is, contrary to the deep-going self-doubt of humanists, in fact quite powerless without a dependence at every step upon irreversible intellection—upon feats of judgment, acts of novel discrimination; upon "imagination."

I read over my argument and still find it—as argument—convincing as a piecemeal exercise. As a humanist however, in this reading, my self-doubts in face of the awesome authority of science are still left untouched by even this cogent argument. It is as if that authority is so deeply ingrained in the intellectual habits of my mindbodily life in this culture that it cannot be chipped away piecemeal—like the argument that there are certain regions of physical theory where the concept of causality is without application; or that thoroughly spurious and slightly desperate argument from Heisenberg's principle of indeterminacy to the reality of human freedom; in other words, what the chemist Charles Coulson has called the theological form of this: the "argument to the

God of the gaps." Such step-by-step argumentation issues in no ecumenic reversals.

Piecemeal arguments, no matter how brilliantly contrived, fail to dislodge the global authority of science because of what Polanyi has called "the principle of suppressed nucleation": Step-by-step arguments, no matter how they are multiplied, cannot nucleate a decisive overturning of a comprehensive mode of human dwelling in the world that is not itself the *product* of science but rather its *progenitor.* To "discredit" science in the narrow sense inflicts no wounds upon this ecumenic view.

When Western humankind came fully into its Judeo-Christian inheritance at almost the very moment that that inheritance began to lose its authority, we found it natural and seductive to begin to conceive of our relation to the world as a more or less exact analogue of God's relation to it, namely, as world transcending creators.

With half our being, becoming more and more obscured by the regnant second-order accounts of our situation in the world and by the whole repertoire of the new modes of our mindbodily life desiderated by those accounts, we went about our quotidian life thoroughly rooted in the world, while with the other and now more authoritative half, we lived the life of discarnate gods. It was this large depiction of our place in the nature of things that gave rise to modern natural science. The reverse side of this exhilarating picture is despair, despair at our alienation from our incarnate actuality.

Romanticism often expressed and sought to come to terms with this despair at our dispossession from the world.

All this being so, drudging, step-by-step assaults upon the imperialistic range of "science," which we have invented because it flatters us, all implications of a kind of intellectual heroism attaching to these efforts aside, is an enterprise with hardly any efficacy, as 350 years of philosophic effort attest.

We will have to turn ourselves right side up, explicitly establishing ourselves on our true foundations: our mindbodily beings in the quotidian world in which we live and move and have our being, of which the second-order world that, though as real as anything can be, is a derivation of this ground. We will have boldly to stake a claim for what we already know full well: the fact of the priority of our incarnate existence.

Having written these words, I ask myself: "And who would deny this?" In this *explicit* form, only the demented. But in this culture we all deny it *tacitly*, since what this culture *explicitly* values and believes entails that we do. My tiresome appeal to my "mindbody" is the reiteration of this necessary bold claim.

8/23/90

If memory, promises given, and promises betrayed are engraven upon my embryonic mindbody, then are not hope and faith?

What precisely is my relation to what I have been calling my second-order account of things. In my eagerness to strike through the veil—an incriminating characterization in itself—it obtrudes between me and my primal actuality, I easily imagine that it is not only second order but second rate, which I do not believe. Yet what is my relation to it? Indeed, what do I mean by *second-order account?*

One way to begin is to try to distinguish between a first-order actuality and a second-order account of it. It may well be that the first and second orders interpenetrate.

It would appear that a distinction between my doing what I did between 9:00 A.M. and noon yesterday (first-order actuality) and a narrative account of this (second-order account) is clear enough. And in a sense it is.

Yet I need to ask whether an *implicit* narrative already informs my doing of what I do, antecedent to any second-order account thereof? I do not refer here to the relatively trivial fact that, if I were asked in the midst of my first-order activity, "What are you doing?" I should be able to say—albeit this already strongly suggests that my second-order narrative on demand is quite continuous with the first-order activity, *logically* continuous—that the logos which tacitly informs my activity endowing my movements through time with continuity and sense (I am not suffering a grand mal seizure) can readily be made explicit by reflection.

8/24/90

Let us suppose that we can, for the sake of analysis, *imagine* (we do not here need to concern ourselves with how this would be viewed by the physiologist) that I stand, upright and quite still in, if you please, an instant without temporal thickness, the several particulars of my musculoskeletal structure having only spatial relations among them, but no temporal ones (excepting the temporal relation of coendurance).

At the moment that this imaginary stasis is brought to an end as I walk across the floor of my living room, these several parts acquire different temporal relations: They *move together* through a certain span of time. (We need to make a distinction here between the time in which *movement* occurs and the "time" in which *static entities endure.*) They have a temporal coherence, grace, and rhythm as they jointly move through the duration of my walk—the more athletic the coherence the more graceful the walk. This coherence of these several musculoskeletal parts (they have ceased to be *parts* immediately upon their integration into my rhythmical walk) throughout the temporal distention of my movements is their logos.

What I have just accomplished in the immediately preceding words is a narrative account—a deployment and representation in the temporal medium of language—of the temporal unfolding of my body in walking. This "second-order" narrative account is achieved by rendering explicit the *implicit* narrative structure of my first-order activity of walking.

If walking as a first-order activity can be said to have an implicit narrative structure, as indeed the very ground for the inference of a *second-order* narrative account, then all the more can we say that what I did between 9:00 A.M. and noon yesterday (It is now day before yesterday) has an implicit narrative structure as the ground of my explicit, second-order narrative account of these doings.

All of this is, I believe, interesting in itself and does constitute a useful amplification of what I have meant here and in my other writings in speaking of the logos that informs our sentience, motility, and orientation, the as-yet-unreflected logos that issues in our reflected life, the common logos that obtains between what I say and the gestures I use as I say it, and so forth. It does not get us much closer however to an answer to the question as to my relation to our second-order accounts, especially those second-order accounts that, I allege, obtrude a veil between me and my primitive actuality.

To advance this analysis, we have to return to the Cartesian dualism of thinking thing–extended thing, the knower and the known.

The second-order account that has rendered us problematic to ourselves is not merely that account of the nature of things begun in the "bifurcation of nature" into, on one hand, mathematically measurable extension and, on the other, everything else that had a merely secondary reality except to the extent that more and more of this latter could be *recovered* by being *reduced* to mensurability; so that, for example, the mind was made identical to the cerebral cortex neurophysiologically understood.

For good and sufficient reasons neurophysiology accomplishes its theoretical goals and performs its prodigies in application only by abstracting itself from the primitive, quotidian actuality of mindbodily life in the ordinary world of sentience, motility, and orientation, commonsensically observed, in order from this detached standpoint to discover that stratum of the lively mindbody that is amenable to interpretation in neurophysiological categories to serve specific and specifically limited theoretical and practical goals.

The promise of the power possessed by natural science to "render us the lords and possessors of nature," when coupled with our millennial tuition to the dogma of the philosophic Enlightenment that that knowledge which is most *secure* because least subject to the hurly-burly of our ordinary life in time is also most true and most valuable, makes it all but impossible for us to measure the appropriateness and limits of, say, neurophysiology. I have had undergraduate students—in theory, though, I trust, not in practice—who found it quite impossible to trust their senses, who steadfastly believe that they were automata and that the colorful world of sensory experience was quite secondary, just as Galileo said, and was to be truly understood only in terms of physics and optics.

This second-order account, the second-order account of natural science since the seventeenth century that is achieved precisely by abstracting us from our mindbodily reality in the primitive world in which we live and move and have our being is that one that makes us problematic to ourselves.

We have seen that, by reason of their joint rootedness in our lively mindbodily beings, there is a continuity between, on one hand, the several degrees of our as-yet-unreflected life and the hierarchy of increasingly abstract forms of reflection in which they may issue, on the other—a continuity that is not likely to be noticed under the suasion of the mind-body dualism.

This being so, it is not easy—or productive—to distinguish between the primary actuality and the derived account as they appear in our practice. It is enough to say that these interpenetrate one another dialectically in our sayings and doings; that even our "commonsense" discourse assimilates the tokens of the second-order accounts produced for us by the values and images of literacy and by the natural sciences.

It is no doubt difficult to say how often or with what "philosophic" effect our casual application to computers of such terms as *memory* and *thought* imports into our conception of "remembering" and "thinking," when applied to ourselves, the sense they have in computerese. The growing insensitivity to this very distinction on the part of many, suggests that the loss is profound, even irreversible.

8/27/90

In a *Philosophical Daybook* I say: ". . . There are analogies among the imaginary/real, fiction/history, figurative/direct, metaphorical/literal, mythos/logos distinctions." And then I later conclude: ". . . Is not having and being in a world precisely to dwell alternately and often richly simultaneously, but never less than *fully,* in both terms of these pairs?"

The implication of this language seems to be—and I believe I thought so at the time I wrote these words—that fiction vs. history, the figurative vs. the direct, mythos vs. logos, and so on offers, in each of these pairs, a distinction between two, in themselves, autonomous and internally coherent modes of discourse that somehow retain their logical integrity even when I, as I suggest above that I do, in actuality dwell alternately and richly simultaneously in both terms of these pairs.

Do my earlier accounts of the relation between *reflection in course* and *detached reflection,* between first-order actualities and second-order accounts of them, between the implicit narrative in my actions and explicit narrative reports on them—wherein in every case, the continuity between the members of every pair is underscored—suggest that this misrepresents the relation *in actuality* between mythos and logos, and so forth? After all, my steadfast conviction is that the figures that, in analysis, form each of the modes of discourse of each term in these binary pairs derive from and retain their meaning and authority only by reference to my mindbody in the world in the midst of my ordinary doings and sayings.

In other words, although it may be necessary, for the sake of the activity in the world of critical reflection, to distinguish between figurative and direct, fiction and history, and so on, it may well be a misrepresentation of the way in which what is *called,* in critical reflection, mythos and logos enter into the formation of the world in which we actually dwell. Indeed, it may be discovered that the way in which the contrasts between imaginary and real, fiction and history, figurative and direct, metaphorical and literal, mythos and logos are *identified* is a function of the requirements and prepossessions of *our* mode at a given moment of critical reflection, that the terms of analysis are not forced upon us by "the facts" but rather serve to sustain and propagate a certain view of ourselves that we deeply cherish.

I want to suggest that *in the world in which I live and move and have my being* what are called mythos and logos, fiction and history, and so forth in critical reflection *do not exist.* (On its face this would seem like a truism.) At a given moment of my apprehension of the world there no doubt enter elements of each of the modes *denominated in critical reflection* by these terms. But in the seamless web of my actual experience these distinctions do not appear as such. Indeed, if they did, the world of ordinary experience would be fragmented and hopelessly confusing.

8/28/90

The words of the Apostles' Creed when, in speaking them, I claim them as my own make a world appear—as palpable as anything can be. Yet viewed from the standpoint of detached reflection, from the standpoint, that is, not of one who professes them but of one who would sort out the strata of its language, the Creed is logically complex. From the perspective from which we approach it as denizens of this culture, its several parts, though brought together in this putatively integral verbal icon (the world that it makes appear is no icon but the thing itself), are governed by different and, it would appear, uncongenial logics.

"I believe in God, the Father Almighty, Maker of heaven and earth." It is entirely possible to subject this sentence to a microanalysis; for example, to distinguish between a belief in *God* and believing in the appropriateness of the predicate "Father Almighty" on the ground that the logic of the latter is problematic as that of the former is not.

For the purposes of this analysis however it will suffice to regard the whole formula as informed by one logic, the logic, namely, of myth. I call this myth not to suggest that there is anything the least bit equivocal in the reality embodied in its language, but rather to underscore my belief that this language has to do, not with astrophysics, but with the ultimate meaning and value for us of the world, the possible nonexistence of which we routinely experience.

By the same token, I regard as having the logic of myth the words: "And in Jesus Christ [not Jesuah of Nazareth, a young rabbi] his only Son our Lord: Who was conceived by the Holy Ghost, Born of the Virgin Mary." I say that this is governed by the logic of myth because in relating an historically identifiable teacher to "God, the Father Almighty" with references to his peculiar sonship, attested by claims of his miraculous birth, this historical rabbi participates in the ultimate meaning and value for us of our existence in history (not discarnate in an eternity).

In saying this, I in no wise imply that this language of myth, of ultimate meaning and value, possesses only an equivocal reality-bearing power. This kind of language is *everywhere* in our discourse because strictly inescapable, even in our most ordinary and offhand references to the future and to hope. The language of the confession of crimes against the Party of the old Bolskevik, Bukharin, is shot through with this kind of "theological" words.

"Suffered under Pontius Pilate, was crucified, dead, and buried." This can be read as straightforward reportage of certain events occurring in a politically volatile Roman colony in Palestine, attested not only in the synoptic Gospels, but in the writings of "objective" historians such as Josephus and Tacitus.

It is probably impossible for us to read the words in this creed with the same conceptual prepossessions as those who first formulated it to fashion limits for the emerging Christian community, surrounded on all hands by a profusion of religious sects. How could our ears, conditioned by the logical matrix of the English language and its etymology, to say nothing of the conceptual environment produced by modern physical science, hear these words as they were heard by those whose linguistic context was some combination or other of Greek, Hebrew, Aramaic?

There is no need to continue this analysis of the Apostles' Creed to an exhausting end. It is sufficient here to observe that in what has already been done there have been juxtaposed what from a detached standpoint is the language of myth and the language of history and that this very juxtaposition brings into being an *integral* formula that is neither strictly the one nor the other.

There is nothing extraordinary about this. On the contrary, our everyday speaking is composed of languages, images, and metaphors that could easily be shown from a detached critical—and of course irrelevant—standpoint to exhibit some logical strain. Doing this never occurs to us in the course of our quotidian speech acts. They quite happily bring forth for us the actual world in which we live.

When therefore I recite the Apostles' Creed as my own, usually in the context of an act of corporate worship, I do not profess it piecemeal but as a logically integral form of words that makes that world in which I live and move appear.

One comes to the end of this with a certain sense of weariness. Who does not already know this? How could we even claim to *know* it, as if it could be otherwise. The answer is, of course, that we all have to work our way back to the common sense of our oral-aural life after the values and images of literacy have superordinated logos over mythos, the allegedly direct over the figurative, the real over the imaginary—and all the rest, distinctions that have no purchase in our ordinary doings and sayings but rather are inventions of our literacy that cause us to lose our footing in ordinary life.

Quite apart from the assignment of a privilege to logos, modeled upon the enduring word of writing, the very existence of chirography and later of print made it possible to assume a detached view upon the "logic of discourse," examining it apart from its integration into acts of speech; indeed, it made such analysis apart from use normative.

8/29/90

To make a point, I earlier on drew a distinction between, on the one hand, the musculoskeletal particulars of my erect body imagined as static entities in an instant without temporal thickness—in an eternity, in other words—and, on the other hand, the temporal relations among these particulars when I walk across the room in the temporal flow of my rhythmical gait.

Elsewhere I have drawn a distinction between the relatively static time of objects enduring in visual space and the relatively fleeting time of a succession of spoken and heard words in the time of oral-aural reciprocity.

Finally, I elsewhere also say that the time during which my body may be said unchangingly to endure as the spatiotemporal background for the movements of my running mindbody is a different time from that in which these motions are occurring.

On their face, these remarks strike me as entirely convincing, since the various ways in which the temporal form of different things in the world is perceived and remarked by the use of the word *time* and its cognates always proceeds from my primitive actuality in the world as sentient, motile and oriented—the omnipresent, radically inalienable, and logically necessary matrix within which all my acts of meaning discernment are conceived and brought to term, no matter how abstracted from this matrix are the vectors by which these acts are borne.

When I proceed on these grounds, the "problem of time" is not some large, abstract question concerning the nature of things, but the always concrete one as to how I shall use the word *time* here and here and here as I discriminate among the various ways in which the world presents itself to me.

The word *time,* the concept 'time'—the sum of the ways in which the word may be used—how does my mindbody devise from its inherence in the world a token with which to make reference to one of the features of that inherence? Here my interest is not in the token as such—time, *temps, Zeit*—but in the reality, or rather in the primitive mindbodily *source,* of these words.

My mindbodily life has a rhythm. The perhaps most archaic form of this, from which all others derive, is the beating of my heart: sometimes, when I am excited or exerting myself, fast; in repose, slow.

My mindbody *comprehends* both the second heartbeat and the first which, in a sense, but *only* in a sense, has already come and gone. In fact of course the first beat pretends the second as the second retrotends the first—and the same can be said of an indefinite number of beats prior to the first and following upon the second.

Because of this tension, this stretching forth and stretching back among the beats of my heart, my mindbody is intentional through and through because intentional at its radix—up and down through the hierarchy of its modes of being. Its existence in the world is tonic; the world in which it is is dynamic. Any mode of thought that depicts the nature of things in terms of static entities standing in static (essentially instantaneously visual-spatial) relations is a complete falsification—like Hume's account of perception, which no one can possibly believe.

My heartbeat tells the time of the world—measuring the endurance of the statically enduring and the fleet passing of the dynamic. This tolling tells—that is, counts and narrates—the world and myself in it and, in so doing, periodizes it. It is not too much to say that *all* periodization derives from this beating heart—whether we speak in terms of nanoseconds or lightyears, of the earth, our solar system, or the vibrations of the quartz crystal in my watch that tolls the time of day; whether of my morning's work or my lifetime, the history of humankind on earth, the universe, or Western culture.

Tolling, telling (as counting, as narrating, as recounting)—no etymological kin—periodization, the singing of songs to lighten the burden of work by imparting a rhythmic order to it—it is from these and many cognate experiences that the conception of time is generated.

My breathing in and breathing out, the pace at which I walk, on the whole uniformly periodized, the rhythm of my speech into which a listener will have to enter, adjusting his or her rhythm to mine, if my words and their meaning are to be comprehended.

Investigating this question of time in a context where the lively sentient, motile, and oriented mindbody is taken as bedrock, we readily see that the periodization of all things in the world derives from and is a modulation of this radical temporality of my being.

8/30/90

In undertaking to show the continuity between the primordial ordinations of our lively sentient, motile and oriented being, on the one hand, and the reflective instruments of our most abstract feats of intellection, on the other, I have claimed that language, our first formal system, has the sinews of our bodies that had them first; that the grammar, the syntax, the ingenuous choreography of our rhetorical engagement with the world, the meaning, the semantic and metaphorical intentionalities of our language are preformed in that of our prelingual mindbodily being in the world.

If this were so, it would also necessarily be the case that the emergence of articulation from our mindbodies would be accompanied by an hierarchy of phenomena that could be detailed by the languages of physics, chemistry, biology, neurophysiology, and so on, as this act of writing in which I am now engaged is accompanied by physiological and neurophysiological particulars. (The relation among these strata of phenomena and among the forms of discourse appropriate to each is, no doubt, in the framework demanded by the philosophical tradition, extraordinarily complex. It need not be however, if we take our stand on the ontological priority of our mindbodies, the logical antecedents of all explanatory models, and thereby grasp the fact, first, that the concepts that issue in physics, chemistry, physiology, and so forth are the very speculative instruments *devised* by these mindbodies to propagate the inquires that arise from their demand for meaning and, second, that therefore these strata of phenomena and the explanatory modes appropriate to each are grounded in and unified by these same mindbodies. What I shall not do is embrace the untenable view that, for example, neurophysiology gives us the bedrock "real state of affairs" in the phenomenon of my words being written on this page.)

The basis of my analysis is however my own mindbodily being in the world, taken as essentially unproblematic, elusive to me only because in its dense familiarity it encroaches upon itself in analysis. Upon this, eschewing the temptation to be drawn away from this primitive existential ground toward the abstractions engendered in the mindbody dualism, I undertake a radically empirical investigation, a phenomenological description of the ordinations and hierarchies of this lively matrix of meanings and feats of meaning discernment as I encounter them in the present actuality of my pretensive-retrotensive mindbody. The logos that I apprehend as embodied in the intentionalities of my immediate mindbodily being is the *same* logos that, *in the same way,* I apprehend in the intentionalities presupposed by formal logic and mathematical heuristics. There can be nothing more radical.

When therefore I say, as I have, that articulated distinctions such as those between the literal and metaphorical, history and fiction, logos and mythos are grounded in tacit distinctions rooted in the as-yet-unreflected appreciations by my mindbody of the ironies already given within the fabric of my primitive worldliness, it is to further this program of descriptive phenomenology.

In suggesting that the contrasts as such between the literal and metaphorical, history and fiction, logos and mythos, and the rest, were *ironies,* I believe I was referring to the sense of there being a certain *noncoincidence,* as there could be said to be such between the words that a person speaks that, on their face, have one meaning, but prove to have a different one in fact. Of the person speaking thus we often say that he or she is being ironical because the meanings of his of her words do not coincide with themselves, and the speaker wishes it so.

I am suggesting of course that even the most primitive forms of my mindbodily life are shot through with these ironies, these noncoincidences. Long before I acquired a native language (indeed, as the condition of my doing so) I apprehended the forms of noncoincidence. I know this to have been the case because though I am now a skillful user of my language, I am even now mindbodily and inarticulately aware of these—out of which my acts of articulation are engendered.

If the distinction between the literal and metaphorical, history and fiction, logos and mythos express articulated forms of noncoincidence, it is because the tacit, unarticulated ironies have been given these particular explicitations. Different planes of the real intersect and collide in the inarticulate life of my mindbody in the world. Out of these intersections and collisions comes articulation.

Articulated ironies gain a purchase upon me then, not because, as the speaker with my fellows of our native language, I live among their linguistic embodiment—though of course I do—but because this kind of noncoincidence has been ubiquitous in my unreflected life, forming the ground of my apprehensions of articulated ones, of irony.

How do I know that this is so? Because the very words that I have been and am just now writing are themselves the articulation of some ironies in the mindbody that brought them forth.

Is this a *petitio principii?* Yes. Nevertheless, pay mindbodily attention—pay attention in your *own* mindbody—to the way my words bite into you! It is not—as our Enlightenment intellectualism would have it, because you have an intellectual grasp of the meaning of these words—as if you were a "clever" computer. Rather you are able to apprehend the "intellectual" meaning of the words because they are *taken hold* of in your mindbody.

(It is worth noting here, a propos the question of the relations among the several strata of phenomena—physical, chemical, neurophysical—and the several modes of discourse appropriate to each—physics, chemistry, neurophysiology—that the logic that underlies the coherence among the concepts of each of the modes *in itself,* strictly observed, does not hold between one such mode and another. There is no *logical* integration of the logic of one mode of discourse with another. Physics does not *strictly* imply chemistry; chemistry does not *strictly* imply biology. Their integration exists *ontologically.* As knowers we integrate in our *mindbodily feat of knowing* what does not cohere *logically* in itself. On the other side, these strata and the discourse appropriate to each as educed by acts of analysis cohere *ontologically,* that is, in the *object* of knowledge before us. We behold an ordinary, commonsense human being, suffering, let us say from a lesion in the frontal lobe (to be exact, we can, at this point, only say that he is given to bizarre behavior). Our several modes of analysis are jointly brought to bear upon this commonsense human being. We begin here, we end here. *This* is what is radical. Otherwise we slip into what Whitehead called the "fallacy of misplaced concreteness."

On the noetic side, the side of the ordinary knowing of this commonsense person, these modes of discourse cohere in the integral but perfectly ordinary commonsense act of recognizing a commonsense "object."

We cannot bear to admit that the act of knowing and the object of knowledge initially arise from and continually refer back to our mindbodies in the world, because this reminds us of our incarnate status and denies to us the consolations of being gods.

8/31/90

The European Enlightenment discovered "religion." Medieval culture, the romanticization of its unity and coherence notwithstanding, did not "have" religion. There were different centers of power—the Church and the secular polity—sometimes in violent opposition, sometimes virtually indistinguishable, sometimes with one superordinate, sometimes with the other. On the whole however, during the high Middle Ages, within the fabric of the medieval culture and its form of life that, in practice—and in sometimes dynamic "political" struggle—the "sacred" centers of power were distinguished from the "secular" centers in terms of the images, values, and practices that informed the whole of medieval life.

To be sure, the rediscovery of Aristotle in medieval Europe precipitated an intellectual challenge to the Augustinian framework that had held for 800 years. For Augustine the opposition between Ancient philosophy and Christian faith was not so acute as it later became, since for him what later came to be designated "revelation" and "reason" were not so much addressed to two different faculties of the soul as rather the objects of two different loves.

It is only a slight exaggeration to suggest, perhaps, that the appearance of Thomas Aquinas's *Summa* is the portent of the Enlightenment to come. This could be said to be addressed to the question of the standing of salvific truth that is mediated through the particularities of contingent history before the universal reason that discloses the truths of nature—not just physical nature, but the whole structure of reality that is accessible to all persons at all times everywhere.

In explicitly formulating and addressing this problem, the distinction between "truths of reason" and "truths of revelation" was heightened. In short, a distinction began to emerge between rational knowledge and faith, between philosophical truth and religious truth, between the life that is subject to natural knowledge and the distinctly *religious* life, that is, the life shaped by revelation.

"Religion" was well on its way to becoming a special form of life in the matrix of the culture where it appears and to being defined by its authorization in the history of the Jews, in all their historical particularity, and in the primitive Christian community formed around the life, teachings, crucifixion, and resurrection of Jesus, in all of his.

When Enlightenment *philosophes* purposed to purge the world of religion and institute the reign of reason, religion could be seen to be *only* that which had derived from the historical experience of a backward, benighted, and—in the view of that arch-Enlightenment anti-Semite, Voltaire—uncouth Jews; namely, Christianity.

This Enlightenment affect is perfectly expressed in Hilaire Belloc's quip: "How odd of God to choose the Jews."

This of course has diverted us, votaries of the most powerful spiritual force in the modern world as we are, from recognizing Enlightenment as the religion of modernity. The Enlightenment critics of the "scandal of particularity" were of course apologetes of the new religion of Reason.

The Enlightenment, then, rejected "revealed religion," taken to be entangled with and corrupted by historical contingency and irrationally accreted tradition, in favor of "reason" and "nature." Released *from* the obscurantism of this taint of particularity, it felt released *into* the clarity of a "reason" and "nature" that it took to be *sub specie aeternitatis,* unconditioned by particularities of time or place (even though no one explicitly makes this outlandish claim), which is to say, it was released into conceptions necessarily abstract, therefore necessarily superficial, in relation to actual feats of intellection. Confidence that this is what had been achieved has gone untested. This is so because of the abstractness of the Enlightenment's rationalism: its assumption that intellection can be dehistoricized at a stroke by an act of will—as Descartes in his *Discourse* supposed. Its form can thus be arrayed before us with total explicitness in an instant on a single logical level; human reason is thought to be conceivable without the traction afforded by historical-conceptual density. It then became unimaginable that historically revealed religion could have had any role in the formation of the concepts 'reason' and 'nature,' now presumed to be ahistorical. This misdescription of reason did not seriously or long inhibit the advancement of science, since its praxis insulated it against this theory. The malign effects appear in philosophy, politics, and the so-called human sciences, where what one believes about human nature is pivotal. The Enlightenment views of reason and nature embody its philosophical anthropology.

In this doctrine reason is, by default, *imagined* though rarely *said* to be discarnate, with results that, when we think about them, strike us as being too bizarre to be believed—even to the point of our denying we believe them; but with which, when we do not think about them, namely, most of the time, we are quite comfortable.

If one operates out of such assumptions, it is impossible not to believe that the logical disaffiliation of concepts of "reason" and "nature" from historical revelation can be achieved on demand. What the Enlightenment desiderated in one moment was in the very next simply declared to be an accomplished fact.

A good deal of what has been written therefore amounts to the Enlightenment interpreting the Enlightenment.

The modern university, the creature par excellence

of *Aufklärung,* has now become the church of this fundamentalist faith.

9/4/90

In the summer of 1970, en route to Stanford University for a stint as a visiting professor, I lay on my back, for six hours, on a large rock on the north rim of the Grand Canyon. When I began, the sun was well past the meridian, westering toward my horizon, brightly reflecting off a rock facing. When I called it a day, the sky was black, punctuated with crystals of starlight.

My purpose was to determine whether it would be possible for me so to reorient my whole mindbodily sensibility, as by contrivance, to look upon the magnitude of this natural phenomenon in a fashion analogous to that that I imagined a Hopi Indian quite naturally might have looked.

At the angle at which I lay, I could, with comfort, look across that great gash in the earth in a west northwesterly direction toward a large shoulder of rock upon which (at a distance of about five miles, as the crow flies), when I began my experiment, caught the sunlight and reflected it in tones of gold, copper, and bronze.

Notice how I have just described my situation. I do not really know how a Hopi Indian would describe this scene—and, in a sense, it is quite enough for me to imagine some depiction of it alternative to what would come naturally to me. I do believe, for example, that he would not speak of *sunlight being reflected off a rock face.* Certainly not in the way I do.

If I were to succeed, I should have to experience the gash in the earth, the shades of light at different levels in this gash, the geologic strata of the opposing rockface, the occasional fleecy clouds, that drifted through my field of vision, the predatory birds that easily rode the thermals, just above the canyon's rim, the sounds of birds and other small wildlife near at hand as all being integral to a vast, ceaselessly evolving organism of everchanging colors in which I am myself submerged.

For these several hours there was the contest in me between experiencing the changing scene as the creature that I am of Copernicanism—science, technology, and the subject-object dichotomy (I really had no difficulty, my Copernicanism notwithstanding, with seeing the sun moving toward the West)—and experiencing it to a degree in what I imagine as the Hopi Indian way.

The contest was *not* between first thinking, that is, saying to myself, things like "Now I am looking at the scene in *this,* natural, modern commonsensical way; the Hopi would not look at it in *that* way, but rather as . . ." I found instead that I began to surrender the hold upon me of my natural way of seeing only as I slipped my *mind-bodily* bonds to that way of dwelling in the world, that I began to approach the way of seeing these things as a vast, living organism and myself as part of it, only when I allowed my lively mindbody to insert itself into the world in this new way. As certainly as I do not dwell *naturally* in the world only or even primarily in explicit ways, but through the total mindbodily investment of myself with its global capacity for discerning meaning by participation, so certainly will I be able to dwell in it as a Hopi only in the same way.

As the sun moved across the western sky—as I should say, abandoning my sense of being a living part of a vast, living organism—the colors on the rock face changed, first to a lavender, then a purple, then blue, then leaden; light receded first from the depths, then from the higher elevations in the canyon; the hawks flew down into the canyon twilight, hunting their prey at just the moment when, for perhaps only a few minutes, the small animals ventured from their daytime hiding places to feed.

For several fleeting moments during my six-hour experiment on the north rim of the Grand Canyon I had a sense of being someone else somewhere else. These moments, for all their fascination—and, indeed, their gift of beatitude—were unstable and evanescent, constantly under pressure, as they were, from what was *natural* to my mindbody in the world, from what had been sedimented there in *our* history and taken up in *my* history, the prehistory and history of my mindbody, the ground for me of all meaning and meaning discernment.

And what philosophic import do I wish to infer from this? Not the modest and passing triumph over relativism, though that is there (but that had already been achieved in my entertaining the belief that the Hopi Indian is enough like me to allow me to plan an attempt to become more like him).

The question that is of interest here is: What is it like to both *have* and be *in the midst of* a culture?

The first thing to be said is precisely that we both *have* and are *in the midst of* our culture!

Descartes gave articulation to values, aspirations, and images of how the human being abides in the world (hardly at all) that had been struggling toward a focus in the European soul for nearly 200 years by the time he wrote his *Discourse* and *Meditations.* Long before Kant wrote his essay "What Is Enlightenment?" Descartes had already given the paradigmatic answer: "De Omnibus dubitandum est"—thinking that this was quite easily done. He did not even come close! Divesting his mind of all his previous beliefs and the teachings of his masters at the school at La Flêche, he nevertheless faltered when he turned to those hopelessly historically accreted instruments, Latin and French, as the vectors of his revolutionary ideas.

It is largely irrelevant that Descartes seems not to have noticed this embarrassment to his sweeping claim. What is of importance is the fact the European intellectuals—and ourselves down to this very day—embraced this as a doctrine they already tacitly held and deeply cherished.

Enlightenment, in consequence, moves us to imagine that we stand to ourselves like God in absolutely lucid acts of reflection (as Descartes imagined he did). The corollaries of this are that only that knowledge of other minds such as God could have can count as *knowledge;* and only that knowledge of other cultures such as God can have can overcome our ethnocentrism.

Since the first premise is clearly false, no matter how desperately we cling to it, the conclusion is false. Descartes, as he aspired to absolute lucidity, could not even notice that he was inextricably entrammeled by the history, etymology and then current usage of Latin and French. Often, perhaps usually, we are so eager to preserve this illusion of absolute lucidity that we simply refuse to grant this Cartesian embarrassment any philosophic weight.

9/5/90

We are *in our* culture and our culture is *in* us. This is a truism; everybody knows it. Yet it is easily overlooked when we formulate the problem of cultural relativism in our frequently overly abstract fashion. Here we seem to view ourselves as denizens of our culture—as we view others as denizens of theirs—according to the Cartesian picture of one who, by a simple, lucid act of will, can identify his or her beliefs, attitudes, values, and grounding in the world in order to forswear them even if, as is claimed, only methodologically. Even though we know this is absurd when we reason closer to the ground, in the mythology of Enlightenment this is the view that we are given. Combine this motif with the image of each one of us as a social atom, a windowless monad, and you have at the level of common sense such remarks as: "Hitler was sincere in his beliefs. Who am I to say?" Frequently the person given to saying such things, out of deference to received opinion in this culture, is at the same time given to the most intransigent forms of dogmatism, not least in the dogma that it is not for him or her to say.

My culture is composed of what might be called the infrastructure of my practical activity in the world, the sum total of all the tools and instruments by means of which I am engaged with nature and my fellows. It is my automobile, public transportation, the filling station, the airline that enable me to go from point A to point B. It is, in short, the artifacts by which I am surrounded.

It is no less however the interests, needs, values that issued in the fashioning of these artifacts and the *other* vectors of these goals that, even though they do not function in my life in the way that tools do, are no less—perhaps even more rudimental and prior—features of my culture.

But of course these artifacts have been appropriated, introjected into the very fabric and rhythm of my mindbodily life—*of our* mindbodily life. All of the operative and active intentionalities of my mindbody even as I sit at repose in my study, encorporate the automobile in my carport as an available potential source of transport, even as they encorporate a dysfunctional automobile, entering into the specific way that time will be structured for me, into the rhythm and pace of my movement, both virtual and actual. Possibility—and impossibility—are for me defined by this. Recall the drastic revision in your mode of mindbodily being in the world precipitated by a blown tire on the interstate. For awhile you live a much more primitive form of life, both actually and in fantasy.

My culture is of course our native language. It is at once the equal, common possession of us all and uniquely mine, when I use it to speak (or write) in my own name.

In the first case our language is the grammar, syntax, semantical resources that are husbanded in our printed books and dictionaries: institutions ancient and historically dense.

But this language as institution resides no less in the lively mindbody for which it is an everpresent resource. Quite apart from my actual acts of drawing on this reservoir in speech, its continuing availability in my mindbodily being enters into the formation of who and what I am; as certainly as the continuing availability of my physical aptitudes do; as certainly as the loss of these do. The culture in which I dwell when suffering from some form of aphasia is a different one from the one I now in fact dwell in.

This language that I have introjected as I acquired it as my native tongue is itself formed of a network of fine roots, not just the usages of my speech community, not just the idioms, not just the concepts and their history—the sum of the ways in which words may be used—disposing me, as I struggle to articulate thought, to move in one rather than in some other direction; it is the history of the language as embodied in its etymology, reaching down through French, German to Latin, Greek, and Sanscrit. And it is the metaphors and analogies that are implicated in this etymology—in the way that words derive from and play upon their likeness to the fundamental ordinations of the mindbody in its sentient and motile orientation in the world; for example, the etymological and metaphorical affiliations of the word *intension* with the quite rudimentary mindbodily act of stretching.

Even when I am silent I bear this lingual culture about in my mindbody. I *am* who and what I am because of this. If I were utterly blind to the etymology of this language, borne about and always at the ready, I would be someone else. There would be things I could not say, could not think, would not feel.

The extent to which it has been possible for me to *detail* the elements constituting my culture, as earlier, I may be said to *have* that culture. The extent to which, at a given moment, I unreflectingly act out of these elements, I may be said to be *in the midst* of it.

There are tacit—even unconscious, in the sense of repressed—elements that defy my efforts to detail them. But they not only lie beyond the power of explicitation, they are *incommutable.* As I live and move and have my being in the quotidian world there are many things that it is impossible for me to doubt—and not just the efficacy of the language that I use to say so.

In my reiterated emphasis upon the capacity—no, the exigent demand—for coherence of my mindbody in its sentient, motile, and self-orienting pretensive-retrotensive life, it appears at times that there is no purchase in the nature of things as I see it for *dissonance*: epistemological, ontological, ethical, religious.

Whether my mindbodily intentionality in its explorations of the real is viewed in terms of its power to devise its own most archaic figures in which to bring forth and embody the objects of its knowledge, or its articulation of the structure of the natural world, or its formalization of the rubrics governing reversible ratiocination, or its flights into the unexplored reaches of pure mathematics; whether its world-forming powers are seen in its feats of imagination—irreversible reasoning—or its capacity to devise the framework for my life in time by reference to first and last things, expressed in myth, or its genius for epitomizing in its rituals the meaning and the structure of time in obedience to the rhythms of the earth. I have represented each of these as pretensions of my integral, lively mindbody in which all these, for all their diversity, cohere; and in turn, severally coherently retrotend this mindbody.

For example, I have earlier distinguished between the time of their endurance of the static physical objects that form the background of my lively activities and the dynamic time in which these activities unfold. All the traditional puzzlement over the question of the "nature of time" dissolves in the recognition that the so-called problem of time is but the question: How shall we *use* the word time in *this* context? And that will be decided by the nature of that modulation of the basic rhythm of my mindbodily being, embodied in my beating heart, which the temporality of the present case is. I claim that all these various uses of *time*, as diverse as they are, cohere in the mindbody of whose intentionality they are variations. Of course this process of integration usually occurs instantaneously and certainly without being remarked. Such is the mastery of the tacit logos of my mindbody.

If the demand for order, coherence, integrity is so exigent, and if this is for the most part achieved instantaneously and without reflection, then is my mindbody not also infallible? Is there any place for dissonance, contradiction, criticism?

When I fetch the morning paper before daylight and "read" its front page as I walk, in the half-light, without my specs, I make perfectly good sense of what I am barely able to see. The first letters in words, their lengths in relation to other words—and given the subject matter defined by the headlines that I *can* see—I devise a sense for what I am reading. Indeed, I cannot help doing so. Failing eyesight, inadequate light cannot stay my demand for coherence and intelligibility—even for the few seconds required to go from the end of the driveway to my lighted kitchen. Inside and bespectacled, I get it right. No explicit criticism is involved. I see the text as it really is; I see *how* what really is lent itself to my earlier and often amusing misconstructions.

Now, in a way this is a perfect paradigm of the style in which my mindbodily life unfolds in the world: demanding and seeking sense, correcting its misconstructions for the sake of a new integration, plunging forward to the apprehensions of new gestalts, correcting these in turn for the sake of a more comprehensive integrity.

In other words, *criticism is ubiquitous.* Seeking coherence is the feat of grasping gestalts, dissolving them for the sake of a more inclusive coherence; dissolving them because they cannot be integrated to a larger more comprehensive one. Criticism is the tacit, mindbodily recognition of incoherence in the course of my quest of coherence. This criticism is incessantly being carried out instantaneously by my mindbody that is the ground and matrix of all meaning and meaning discernment, of order, coherence, and value.

All of my immediately foregoing reflections, while at every step relying upon the unreflected criticism that goes on unobserved, are, in various ways, criticism as well: *explicit* criticism.

At the end of almost every morning's writing I have succeeded in producing another installment of that critique of dualism that has engaged me now for more than forty years, coming at the incoherences I have apprehended from yet another direction, by means of criticism both tacit and explicit, overcoming the disorder that is the work of this culture's grossest incoherences.

And yet usually when I begin there is at first no anticipation of an agenda of explicit issues upon which to bring the instrument of critical, reversible ratiocination to bear. Often there is nothing more than the commitment to seat myself in my study chair, pen and open notebook in hand, with the purpose of placing myself through what I write in a better relation with myself and the world.

Too often, it seems, I sit in a vague state of unease, aware that there is a something-I-know-not-what demanding to achieve explicit embodiment; all of this made more acutely discomfiting because I hear "time's winged chariot at my back."

From experience I know there is yet another species of incoherence in the texture of my mindbody, born of the large incoherence of dualism, urging its critique, struggling into words. Something nags. I feel awkwardly placed in the world.

Finally, not knowing where this will go, I simply begin to write. That inchoate sense of disorder that is the critic of the incoherences in my being finds a voice, a language.

This unease that has pervaded my intellectual life for more than forty years has been the tacit critic of the culture in which I have been called upon to live my life. And as I have dwelt with this it has been formulated as the incommensurabiltiy between, on one hand, the second-order account of the nature of things devised in the development of the natural sciences and, on the other, the first-order life I live, in which I move and have my being, between the world of literacy with its values of linearity and stasis and the world of our residual oral-aural reciprocity.

If I have not been rendered completely dysfunctional by this incommensurability (have I not?), if this culture has not broken in half (has it not?), it is because of the genius of my mindbody—of our convivial mindbodies—for overcoming in practice the split that in theory—that is, within a detached point of view—will not heal.

A neurotic construction of reality is after all a coherent view of things; coherent and therefore, for as long as it overcomes its repressed incoherence, efficacious.

Psychoanalysis may be said to be a form of criticism that would dissolve an incoherent view in favor of a new coherency. And the analysand exchanges the one for the other when, with the support of the analyst, appropriating the new coherency as his or her own—when, that is, appreciating it as a new *coherency.*

From this point of view, from the point of view, namely, of these reflections, is not "psychosomatic illness" the mindbody's critique of its own incoherences?

As Pascal said, "It is natural for the mind to believe and for the will to love, so that for want of true objects they must attach themselves to false."

9/7/90

I came to several reflections upon reading Richard Niebuhr's *Faith on Earth,* the theological essay that I find most congenial to my own investigations.

For both Niebuhr and me reflection always begins and ends, because it is ineluctably rooted, in the self—that concentering of the integral mindbody when it is fully responsive to "an otherness that can say I"[n]—richly implicated with the world.

For me this self is experienced at bottom and throughout the hierarchy of its modes of being as a pretensive-retrotensive mindbody, concentered and defined by the momentary object of one of its pretensions.

For Niebuhr the self is experienced at bottom and throughout the hierarchy of its modes of being as a fiduciary structure (*fides, fiducia, fidelitas*)—as the responsive-responsible self.

The dynamic intentionality at the heart of our existence, if prescinded by detached reflection from the temporality that infuses its whole being, easily disappears into the static dualisms that we readily forget are derivative. We become the prisoners of our own reflectively induced amnesia.

Though the problem of dualism is not the focus of Niebuhr's attention, as it is of mine, his thought, no less than mine, is antidualistic in its import. He has, as I have, radically shifted away from the ground upon which dualism arose and upon which it has thriven and this by taking his stand upon the self before God.

For me dualism is healed by being shown to be derivative of the bedrock pretensions and retrotensions of our convivial mindbodily being. For Niebuhr, by implication, dualism is overcome by being shown to be derivative of the bedrock, dynamic fiduciary structure of the self.

This means that neither for Niebuhr nor for me is the distinction between philosophy and theology any

---

[n]W. H. Auden.

longer a fruitful, or even tenable, one. After all, this distinction is the invention of the philosophical tradition that took the investigation of abstractions employing reversible reasoning as practiced by philosophers to be normative for "rational" reflection as such (whereas we can now see, in view of the tacit logos that is omnipresent in our quest for meaning and coherence and in view also of the ubiquitous and necessary operation of irreversible reasoning and judgement in *all* our reflection, how constricted and parochial such an understanding is), thereby ruling that "religious" claims, rooted in orality—in other words, in the relationship between God who speaks to us and we answer—were in principle problematic.

This of course issued in all the familiar dualisms that define and, as I hold, plague theological inquiry: reason-revelation, knowledge-belief, nature-grace, and so forth.

If it becomes desirable in the doing of theology to use these and cognate notions—and I believe it will—it *cannot* mean that, let us say, reversible reason and its objects will be taken to have more substantial grounding than what is said to be "revealed." This distinction will have different work to do, the terms, *equally derived* as they are from the figuring powers of our mindbodies as grounded in themselves in all their intractability, articulate for us a coherent world, refer to *equal modes* of our pretensions toward the real. The logic of these several modes of our pretensions—natural science, poetry, mathematics, law, "common sense," historiography, myth, "revelation," and so on—are of course very different from one another, but not in the respect that some are well-grounded, whereas others are grounded not all: They all have the *same* ground, the *same* reality bearing authority, when they are evaluated, as I am throughout claiming they ought to be, from the standpoint of our primitive mode of dwelling in the world.

This of course means that the Kantian distinction between *Wissenschaft,* which, though strictly circumscribed, is well-founded, and faith, which the circumscription makes possible (according to Kant), cannot hold. This is but the most prestigious eighteenth century version of the seventeenth century dualism that we have come to see is parochial in the extreme. Our intellectual enterprise must begin at an ontological ground zero.

9/10/90

But does not this reconstitution of the relation between reason and faith really deprive theology of one its "theological virtues," namely, the virtue of faith; or more exactly, does not drastically limiting the scope of the Kantian distinction (within which "faith" was in any case secured) produce a strange and indeterminate amalgam into which both faith and reason disappear as species disappear into their genus?

It will appear so as long as our conception of the possible uses of the words *reason* and *faith* are subject to the suasions, however subtly, however attenuated, to Plato's analogy of the divided line in *Republic,* 509eff. Here is established an hierarchy of four "affections of the soul" corresponding to four objects of these affections: *intellection* corresponding to "unmediated" pure ideas; *understanding* in reasoning from unsupported premises; belief in *opinion* about the ordinary world of accepted common sense; mere *sensation* relying on the sensible.

This hierarchy of epistemic modes and their objects, with pure intellectual *vision* of the unchanging forms at the top—all the other modes and their objects descending from *epistéme* in clarity of apprehension and declining reality—is the perfect "epistemological-ontological" embodiment of the new images and values of alphabetic literacy.

What is germaine here is that belief—*pistis,* usually translated "faith" in the New Testament—is next to the bottom in this "epistemological" grading, with intellectual vision at the top, just one step up from mere sensation of the fugitively sensible.

Whatever else 'faith' in its various uses has meant, it was almost always tainted by this suggestion that it is an inferior grade of knowledge—even that it is the *antithesis* of knowledge. Even the characterization of faith in Hebrews XI, "now faith is the substance of things hoped for, the evidence of things not seen," is interpreted in accordance with the analogy of the divided line—as if Hebrews XI were making a kind of epistemological claim, rather than giving a description of an orientation of trust and loyalty toward God as we live our lives; and of God as never-failingly faithful toward us *in time.*

It is a precarious business trying to compare the modes of thought in classical antiquity with those of biblical thought. A good deal of treachery lies in store for our unwary use of *epistemological* and *ontological.* Indeed, it is seriously to be wondered whether we can, without severely misleading ourselves, speak of alternative views of "the problem of knowledge" in Greek and Hebrew thought. Between these two there is no *common* "problem of knowledge." If the problem of knowledge comes, in the end, to a quest for certainty, defined as the grasp of an unchanging reality by the soul most fully untrammeled by the exigencies of our carnal nature in time, itself affording no noetic purchase, there is little or no comportability in this with that kind of "knowing" upon which we rely in our quotidian life amidst the contingencies of time—not a form of knowing that we are forced to settle for, since, alas, we have no other; nor yet a knowing that is "the best we've got." This knowing in time of our life in time is *as efficacious as any we could conceive;* and as we rely upon it from one moment to the next, it is as certain, as trustworthy as anything could be.

My argument then, far from depriving theology of its unique "theological virtues," places the questions far deeper than Kant, who would make room for faith by circumscribing reason.

In my life I am given to infidelity, always ultimately toward God; I am disloyal, justifying those who would say that I am not to be relied upon; I am untrusting, fearful, always ultimately toward God, but proximately toward my neighbor; I falter, lose hope in my eternal significance, fall into despair, the sickness unto death, the black hole of nihilism.

These are not the result of failures of *knowledge,* understood in terms of Plato's analogy of the divided line nor can the malady be overcome by knowledge, so construed.

We all know this perfectly well who have ever been "consoled" by well-meaning friends who would overcome our despair by enjoining us to achieve a higher form of noesis.

The theological virtues of faith and hope have their bearing here. They are the marks of the way we live from one moment to the next, to the next, in loyalty or disloyalty to God.

Previously I made the claim, outlandish even to me as I read it over after the event, that Niebuhr has overcome dualism, as I have, by radically shifting away from the ground upon which it arose and upon which it has thriven, *and this by taking his stand upon the self before God.* What possible difference could this make? What does such a claim amount to?

To unpack all this it will be necessary to animadvert upon a notion I develop elsewhere,° namely, the notion of a *theater of reflection.* "When I interrupt the flow of my ordinary practical activity in the world in order to reflect, I will find both myself and the objects of my curiosity presented in a certain fantasy-setting, upon some particular stage, in some singular theater both *in* which reflection *is given* and *upon* which reflection is *brought to bear.*"

It was Descartes who articulated the paradigmatic theater within which Enlightenment reflection was depicted as taking place. In his view of himself in a solitary room in Germany during the winter, enjoying, as he imagined, an absolutely lucid relation to all his received beliefs, answerable only to himself and his ecumenic doubt that this very depiction of himself made seem possible, he formulated the conception of a discarnate *cogito* in a theater of solitude. This is quite plainly what Descartes said, even though his spare picture was mitigated by all that he—and indeed more than a century of thought—surreptitiously supplied, to render coherent what on its face was incoherent. This godlike *cogito,* lucid to itself, transcendent of itself in its theater of solitude is not defined in any way by its relation to an opposing personal other. The Cartesian God as a religious reality is bracketed before the program of ecumenic doubt is launched. The God of Descartes's philosophy is nothing but the God of the philosophical proofs, as Pascal saw. The theater of solitude comes to ground in Hume's

°See Appendix, pp. 194–203.

inability either to avoid or wholly embrace the conclusion that the self was empty, nothing but sensations of this and that; Kant's rescue operation for the *cogito,* giving it some weight and substance by confronting it with the grandeur of the moral law, was a half-measure that never quite restored what was lost in the *Critique of Pure Reason.*

So-called poststructuralist criticism drawing its energy from Hegel and Heidegger, transacts its business unrepentant, in this theater of solitude.

The picture of a solitary reader confronted by a printed text, its words existing in an "eternity" when compared with the dynamic forward surge of speaking and hearing speech in the oral–aural reciprocity is that of discarnate intellection in an essentially *aesthetic*—that is to say, having a *humanly* noncommittal—relation to its objects. In contrast with this aesthetic relation to printed words, for me just to *listen* in good faith to what you say in good faith, never mind the profounder contracts between you and me that may be tacitly and explicitly negotiated, is for me to move toward an ethical relation to that other by which I am here confronted. In so doing, I draw all the powers and intentionalities of my mindbodily being to a focus and toward a concentering in covenantal speech and transcendence. It is for me, in this confrontation, to be a person before a person.

Depicting myself as a *cogito* in a theater of solitude makes it possible—*makes it probable*—that in my feats of abstract intellection I will quite overlook the rich reality of my incarnate mindbody, upon which in its sentient, motile, oriented being no dualism can arise. When, by contrast with the aesthetic relation I have as the solitary reader of an eternal text, I experience myself as *this* mindbodily being, concentered in my incarnate self before the *I will be that I will be,* even as Abraham, I dwell in *my* ground in *its* ground—where no dualism can gain purchase.

This is what it means to say that Niebuhr and I have shifted away from the ground upon which dualism arose and has thriven by taking our stand upon the self before God.

9/11/90

Judaism and Christianity, with their faithful affirmation of the goodness of the created world—as well as those morbid hypertrophications of these, in various forms of gnosticism that abound even, indeed especially, to the present day, with their denial of creation's goodness—made us into transcendent spirits in our covenant with Yahweh in speech exchanged, in which, whether faithful or not, we are bound to him.

When our fealty to the Creator and the world that he has made was attenuated to the breaking point, we were, as spirits, bereaved of both the ground of our mindbodies in the good creation, from which our unique acts of speech transcended, and of the God in speaking with whom our transcendence was accomplished. Thus, grounded neither in our mindbodily incarnation in the world nor in a covenant with the paradigmatic person, we become abstract spirits, wraiths, rampant in the world, at once everywhere and nowhere, growing more demonic as our fiercely reticent spiritual denial of spirit has sought for a ground in itself.

In the nineteenth century Nietzsche in his way and Kierkegaard in his saw that demonic spirit, loose in the world, is absolute denial, is nihilism. Who can fail to notice the nihilism that lurks just beneath the surface of modern life?

In *The Sickness Unto Death* Kierkegaard wrote: "The formula that describes the state of the self when despair is completely rooted out is this: in relating itself to itself and in willing to be itself, the self rests transparently in the power that established it."

Nietzsche resolved his desperation in the Will to power and the doctrine of eternal return. Kierkegaard proposed to *acknowledge* what he took to be the ultimate truth: whether consumed by the sickness unto death or in trust, we stand before God.

It seems a great distance indeed from the alienation of spirit to the philosophical anomalies of mind-body dualism yet the gnostic denegation of the worth of what is *given*—in the form of what we learn from our own past experiences and at the feet of our masters, and in the resolve to create ourselves *de novo* in a feat of ecumenic doubt—is deeply implicated with Descartes's thought and has its source in that spiritual restlessness, a growing sense of groundlessness, that S. K. professed to see embodied in the legendary figures that portend the end of the Middle Ages: Don Giovanni, Faust, and the Wandering Jew. And this of course is the religion of modernity.

At this point Kiekegaard is my mentor. It was he who authorized for me my own profoundly apprehended sense that I exist before God; and in doing this he enabled me to discover my sentient, motile, and oriented mind-body in the world from which, in authentic acts of speech, I transcended, providing me with the ground upon which at its radix no dualism could find a purchase, thereby supplying me with a foundation from which to define and attack the dualisms of the seventeenth century.

But how can I possibly make so bold, not to say reckless, an assertion in an intellectual setting in which I myself have argued that all the supports for this are eroded, all guidelines down? How can I stake a claim in behalf of a grounding for the self among my fellows who by my own account are deracinate? How can this asseveration be said to strike bedrock?

It is a premise for me that no matter how alienated, even with moral exigency, from the world that, as we conceive it, imposes strictures upon our world-transcending spirits; however alienated, too, from our incarnate mindbodies through which the "fallen" world of our gnostic faith inflicts its ultimate humiliation upon us in our mortality, the express images, values, and implied eschatologies of scientism and technology of the official faith of modernity—a cruel and relentless orthodoxy—cannot wholly repress the ubiquity of Being in our midst, no matter how clandestine must be explicit acknowledgments of its omnipresence.

The Being, the nonexistence of which is inconceivable; that everywhere asseverates itself in all our quotidian doings and sayings, that is therefore historical through and through, in which nevertheless the whole of our mindbodily lives are convivially grounded in the pertinacious substantiality of our pretensions and retrotensions, is the provenance of reality and truth, coherence and value—apart from which no single declaration of our modern faith could be made.

When therefore I declare that I am grounded in myself before God—as ingenuous a phenomenological description of such a fact as I am able to give—I find nothing inherently problematic, either epistemological or ontological, that would not characterize every single fundamental ground we might select (Wittgenstein observed, "If the true is what is grounded, then the ground is not *true,* nor yet false") that would not characterize any ground upon which we would undertake to impeach my claim.

This claim will of course strike many readers as peculiarly problematic, not simply because they do not apprehend it in themselves as carrying conviction, but because, as a reflex, they will take it to be "religious" in nature—as in a sense it surely is, albeit "religious" in the economy of concepts of these investigations and not in that of the Enlightenment that is here under systematic revision.

As we have seen, "religion" for the Enlightenment—I ignore here the Enlightenment as *itself* the religion of reason—was the "preposterous" claim of Christians and Jews that God made his appearance in their historical life. Therefore in our ethos the enunciation of the fundamental premise—my thought is grounded in my self before God; that *I,* a historical being, may stand before God, who appears before me as I before him as the keeper of my responsibility and the endorser of my being; and as the radix from which all my existence and reflection issue forth—such a premise is seen as demanding the most strenuous feats of justification; that is, if it is not dismissed out of hand a priori.

When I think as the creature of the Enlightenment that I off and on am, I am likely to say to myself: "This premise of yours may be an interesting because rather quaint biographical fact about yourself, but highly parochial in its range as it is, dependent upon the contingent historical circumstances of ancient people, of whom there remain but a dispirited remnant, and in no case claiming to be grounded in a universal reason. How can such a premise be of *more* than merely biographical interest?"

If we begin however to see that the doctrine of universal reason—as this was fashioned in the Europe of the eighteenth century (as rooted in the contingencies of historical experience as it necessarily was, therefore as parochial as anything can be); and if we see that the Enlightenment religion of reason was itself an historical "invention" to replace the "discredited" religions of historical revelation, then, without trying to assimilate the logic of the root premise from which these reflections proceed and without supposing that my premise is widely shared; remembering too, what I have sought to establish here, namely, that since all our reflective intellection depends upon the unreflected and operative intentionalities of our mindbodies, rooted in the culture that we at once *have* and are *in the midst of;* we cannot perform an act of lucid choice of what will be the incommutable premise or premises that will be the ground of our thought. Each of us stands where he or she *must* stand, and *having* to stand there is its own justification.

You may find the premise from which my investigations proceed quite uncongenial—and it is certainly not a matter of taste. But if you do, it will not be because it will have failed some simple logical or ontological test that can be readily made explicit.

The Enlightenment distinction between religions of revelation and the religion of reason has its roots in the Platonic distinction between logos and mythos, between what, in Plato's view, was the highest knowledge vouchsafed in the intellectual contemplation of the eternal logoi, on one hand, and the belief in true opinion, falling short of truth by virtue of its "ontological" corruption in its entanglement with the world of coming into being and passing out of being; corrupted too by the fact that the believer in true opinion is not yet intellectually elevated above the contaminations of his or her carnal nature.

No *grounds* for preferring this distinction as the premise for thought could be cited (perhaps the most that could be said is that Plato persuaded emergently literate men of the superiority of the models and values of literacy that they had already begun to introject) as also no such *grounds* could be cited for holding to the Enlightenment's version of this. It was of course the propagation and triumph of alphabetic literacy that carried the day.

9/12/90

Hannah Arendt, if I read her aright (I have in mind here *The Human Condition*), wishes to establish our human uniqueness as transcendent spirits in our acts of authentic speech that is itself the paradigm of 'action'. All other activities called *actions* derive their sense as such from their logical affiliation with speech.

She undertakes to do this however, while, it appears, studiously avoiding an embrace of the premise of herself as grounded in her self before God, even though at the crucial step in making her case she quotes extensively and, I believe takes as her own, passages from Augustine's *Confessions* in which Augustine, in the vocative mood, addresses questions to God as to *what* he (Augustine) is and *who* he is: the earliest in Western *philosophy* to understand his reflection as grounded in a colloquy with God. Having made this quite explicit reference to this episode in the *Confessions,* Arendt has almost nothing more explicitly to say of it, even though her thesis cannot be made without the premise of Augustine's colloquy with God. In short, the conception of the self that appears to be crucial to her can be only the person before God.

To examine her argument *manqué* and juxtapose it to what I have been saying will perhaps cast the gravamen of my own argument in bolder relief.

One concern of her argument is this: How can we establish the hierarchy labor, work, and action in such a way as to ensure the uniqueness of human being among all animal species?

The labor process, like the cycles of nature itself, like all subhuman species in their emergence from nature into life, to pass through their life cycles, to return again to nature, has neither beginning nor end. (Obviously her thought at this point is Greek in inspiration. There is here an eternal cosmos, no doctrine of creation.)

The activity of work issues in *works* that, in contrast to the products of labor, possess a measure of relative durability, surviving the life cycle of perhaps many generations of human beings.

This being so, when we are born (only human beings are *born,* for only they emerge from the eternal cycles of nature) we enter a *world* (as opposed to cyclical nature's never-ending, never-beginning process). This world—not the planet earth, not our solar system, but the *works* of the hands of humankind who preceded us—were already here when each of us arrived and were the condition of our birth (the enduring background of the world that our hands have made provides the context for the appearance of the new); and it will be here when we depart. On this account we celebrate our births and bury our dead.

The activity of work has a specifiable beginning and end. Therefore the work of human hands that is the world is opposed to the eternal cycles of nature and the labor process.

Action—the activity of speaking in the medium of our mutual native language, projected into the world upon the breath of *life,* now become the breath of *speech,* our lively speech as we personally *own* and *stand behind* it—action is the activity by which we appear in the world that our hands have made as something, or rather someone, absolutely new, unpredictable, and unrepeatable.

To be a person, then, is to be *who* we are over and above *what* we are as our being is defined by all the class terms that could be predicated of us—even over and above the class term for a class with only one member, for example, "the person writing the very words that now appear on this page" or "the bearer of the proper name William H. Poteat"; to be a person is precisely to appear in the world as a speaker owning one's words *and to be taken* up in what one says by other persons.

"Spoken words" become words only as they are heard, endorsed as the speech of another's appearance before one and thereby uptaken. Otherwise they are but "words, words, words." My words thus become the vectors of my world-transcending spirit to the extent that they are taken up by you.

Yet, as Arendt is at pains to show, of all human activities speech is the most futile. The presentation of my personhood in the very particular act of expelling my words on the breath of speech, owning my words before others on particular occasions, is, compared to the durable works of our hands and even the perishable products of labor, the most futile of all activities. It does not prosper the immortality of the species nor make and preserve the world. It is just a breath on the wind that is blown away.

9/13/90

How are we to rescue this futile, transient breath from meaninglessness? (It is true, my breath bodies forth my *words*. Surely breath that is the bearer of *words* is not so evanescent as *mere* breath. The issue here however is this: I make my unique, unrepeatable appearance in the world—in, that is, the human context fashioned by the hands of humankind—by bodying forth, owning, and standing behind my *words*, these quintessentially *human* entities, because my unique appearance here is an appearance *as human*—I do not "appear," for example, as a noisy primate; if I were to remain forever *silent*, able but lacking the courage to speak, rather than *mute* by reason of some impediment beyond my control, I should never make a unique *human* appearance in the world; though it is *words* that are bodied forth by the breath of speech, it is not *what* I say that manifests my *unique* appearance in the world but *that* I say my words, own and stand behind them—after all *what* I say may be identical with *what* you say—that is the differentia.)

Clearly, in uniquely bodying forth my words I not only *appear* in the fact *that* I speak, I become entangled in the affairs and history of the world by reason of taking responsibility and being held accountable for *what* I say. No words that I can *now* say nor any that I might be reported as saying in some future document or in some oral narrative of my words and deeds can *express* and *preserve*—make an enduring part of the world—my unique act of novelly saying and owning my words, even if, in the first case I make references to myself as the speaker with the reflexive pronoun *I*, or in the second case the narrator says, "Poteat said . . ." My ownership of my novel utterance that can occur *only* because you take them for such and, for your part, endorse my act of uniquely appearing in them constitute an "event" that *cannot appear in the world,* defined as what can be said in language. It "appears" in the in between of, on one hand, a particular speaker, uniquely appearing as the author of his or her words, opposed, on the other, to a particular hearer who uniquely acknowledges the owned words of the other as the unique marks of his or her appearance. Even though this is the *absolutely* concrete "event," too dense for the abstractions of language to embody and therefore transcends *from* the world, it is a commonplace too ordinary to be wontedly remarked wherever men and women speak and listen to speech—conspicuously of course in the lively reciprocity of our oral-aural life, not so readily noticed or noticed at all where the values of reading and the printed word prevail.

This being so, Arendt's attempt to rescue speech from meaninglessness in its transient futility as the mark of our being as unique persons, fails. For this purpose she reclaims the Greek *polis* as the means for providing other persons to hear and take up one's words, hence consolidating one's human reality over against *homo laborans* and *homo faber.* It is in the memory, so she holds, of those hearers of our words as we speak in the polis and in the stories that they come to tell that, since *who* one is is implicated with one's remembered words and deeds, one's uttered and lively words are rescued from futility. Thereby is one immortalized in one's words and deeds.

We have seen however that *who* I uniquely am paradigmatically appears *only* when, standing in my own mindbody in our mutual world, I speak and am heard by another *living* person on particular occasions in actual historical time, even though this ultimately personal appearance is of course necessarily *affiliated* with, *implicated* in what I in particular have said and done, am given to saying and doing, have thought, fantasized, and dreamed, and with the remembrance of these, by me, by you; with my particular body in its course through its life cycle; with the dense history, culture, and tradition in which I am ensconced and out of which I speak. (These overdetailed qualifications and demurrers I insert to defeat any charge of crypto-Cartesianism.)

Who I am, not to be reduced to the sum of all that can be predicated of me as a certain species of *what* is fully manifested only in my speaking, owning my words, and being taken up as such by another. In short, I can appear as *who* I uniquely am only in an existentially *actual* polis, a gathering of living auditors present and prepared to take me at my word.

Arendt's proposal to immortalize the unique person that I am in stories embodying my words and deeds thus fails, since, though who I am as the *unique author* of my words is implicated with the words I speak and the deeds I do, implicating me in the web of human history, my *unique authorship* transcends the words I speak, abiding for a time between me and those living others who in the space between us as transcending spirits endorse my uniquely appearing self. A fictive or now dead speaker cannot speak with his or her own breath; a fictive or now dead hearer cannot hold me to account or take up what has been said (Hamlet may "take up" the words of Polonius; but this is not at all the same as Olivier taking up the words of John Gielgud!)

Who I am, in the requisite sense, cannot appear in a fiction or in a narrative of my words and deeds. The eternal significance of my unique personhood cannot be exhaustively embodied in either stories or histories.

And yet, unless I have grossly misread Arendt, it is her wish and essential to the program of *The Human Condition* to embrace the view of what constitutes unique personhood just sketched out. No other interpretation enables us to make sense of her allusion to the quotation from Augustine's *Confessions.*

How then is my eternal validity—the phrase is of course Kierkegaard's—to be secured? A polis, during the historical moments of its actual existence, its participants during this time providing, in their readiness to hear and take up my authentic acts of speech, the space within which my words may appear *as words,* apart from which my words are mere blind surds—this polis is at best a transient thing and the space of my appearance may be said to dissolve when the participants adjourn to other activities.

The case, as we have seen, is more equivocal if my being is thought to be preserved in the stories recounted of my words and deeds in later times. My unique appearance as spirit in my *act* of speech (not in a *report* on my act of speech) has not the requisite space in which to "be." The story of "iron-hearted, manslaying Achilles"—perhaps four millenia old—enjoys longevity, but Achilles' "rage" is not the rage of Achilles in an actual space of human appearance, but a fiction. It is no exaggeration to answer the question, "who is Achilles?" by saying, "he is the sole member of the logical class defined by the sum of the terms of Homer's narrative." As such, he is not a person but an abstraction. Even the Jesus whose story is told in the synoptic gospels only appears *as an actual existential presence* as the Son sitting on the right hand of the eternally present Father and in the wine and bread, transubstantiated for the faithful, of which Jesus says: "This is my body which is broken for you; this is my blood which is shed for you." The Eucharist is no fiction.

Then you believe in the doctrine of transubstantiation? Well, no. What I believe—and I do not think of it as something I *believe,* it goes much deeper than that, in fact, all the way to the bone—is that the bread and wine are the *presently actual* body and blood of Jesus Christ; and that, if they are not, then the Son of God has nothing to do with the concrete person I am in *this* time and place; and if this be so, the whole of Christianity is but an elaborate system of symbols at no point engaged with the actual fabric of this world.

9/14/90

In his *Confessions* Augustine takes his stand in his self before God: before a God to whom, in the posture of prayer, he can address the questions of his deepest perplexity; from whom, in answer to these, he waits in patience for reply. In this sustained prayer Augustine appears in the words of his authentic speech in the space in which the answering speech of the supreme person will meet, endorse, and enlighten him.

In so disclosing himself, in speaking vocatively to Yahweh, Augustine at once transcends *from* the world and establishes his eternal validity as incarnate spirit in covenant with him who gives as his name "I will be that I will be."

The unique person that, it appears, Hannah Arendt would oppose to *homo laborans* and *homo faber* can be conceived only in the new kind of "polis" that is first brought into being when Abraham makes covenant with Yahweh and that Augustine introduces into the mainstream of Western philosophical thought, where it has persisted, though perhaps with growing desuetude, as a hidden premise of our thought and action, even to this day.

Only an ongoingly contemporaneous history in which a living and personal being is always actually appearing in the fabric of my present action and speech; who hears and takes up my words and deeds, holding me to account; and who, finally, is taken himself or herself to be faithful, from generation to generation the same can provide the space in which I may appear as a unique incarnate spirit and discover my eternal validity.

9/17/90

I read these thoughts over from time to time while I am still in the course of writing a given day's installment and I find that, long after those habits of thought instilled in me by the dualisms of literacy have lost their power over my imagination, the reflexes persist of thinking that what I have written is some form of idealism.

Occasionally it is obvious that the infelicity of my language is to blame: I have not been sufficiently careful in anticipating the way in which a literate reader will construe my words, taking them to support a form of idealism for which the "real" is nothing but our ideas.

The standing rebuttal to this construction are my reiterated attempts to draw the reader into an apprehension of his or her essentially unmediated ensconcement in the radical, intractable, and in important ways, oppugnant reality of his or her sentient, motile, and oriented mindbodily being in the world that, as reflection emerges, will be appreciated as the ground of all meaning and meaning discernment. Within the ambit of this primitive ubiquitous oppugnancy for each of us, elementary distinctions may begin to emerge and achieve articulation. The distinction between *real* and *ideal*—the sense of "only in the mind"—will not, cannot, be one of them. This distinction has its definitive articulation in the contrast between the "eternal" stability of alphabetic writing, on the one hand, and the "transiency" and hence equivocal reality of words in our oral-aural life, on the other. And of course it becomes in the thought of the seventeenth century the contrast between *real,* intractable, mensurable physical objects and fluctuant sense experience and the meretricious addenda of the "mind."

If we begin with our convivial mindbodies in the world as the given, then the so-called problem of idealism that has been the creature of our literacy—made superordinate over the ongoing asseverations of our oral-aural life—does not arise.

When therefore I revisit passages in my own writing and wince at "finding" myself to be an idealist, I realize that *this* reflex reading of what I have said is one of the last of my bad old habits to die; and I can conclude only that it is likely to be so with you as well.

Is it an embarrassment to me so routinely to appeal to the world in which I live and move and have my being, to the reality and value that asseverate themselves ubiquitously in the fabric of my quotidian life, to my mindbodily being in the world, *while appearing to be quite unable to give instances of each of these in themselves?* What after all *is* an asseveration of reality and value in my quotidian life? How does my mindbody appear in the world? So close at hand in the foreground does it appear that it is not noticed and even when noticed cannot be clearly focused upon—like the visible object too close to our eyes to be clearly seen. The sentences that I have just written and you have just read and are even now still reading embody asseverations of reality and value, in their express meaning, of course, but also, and more powerfully, in the sinews of the etymologies of their words. The metaphorical intentionalities[p] formed in the roots of language already embody an *ur*world whose coherence and meaning imply being and value, whether reflected or not. Their lexical bondings within this temporal density of words are the *atomic* structure of meanings that is implicated in the *molecular* structure of meanings that shapes our sentences. Because of this, being and value are relentlessly asseverated in all our quotidian doings and sayings. And this process goes on incessantly: I, writing or speaking (in which acts of writing and speaking I asseverate); you, incessantly reading, hearing, and responding (in which acts you apprehend asseverations of reality and value and endorse or counterasseverate them in turn). And *as the ground of the meaning and the intentionality of my asseverations,* my mindbody is in the foreground, too close at hand readily to be perceived.

My mindbody however also always appears "at my back." The asseverations of reality and value that are expressed through the preceding sentences I have written and you have read, in all their particularity, have as their provenance my mindbody that is "at my back," in which all its pretensions and retrotensions cohere, forming the world in which these asseverations have their ground and from which they derive their substantiality.

There is embarrassment in this appeal to asseverations of reality and value, only if the test of probity is that of the philosophical tradition that I am undertaking to impeach.

---

[p]See *Polanyian Meditations,* pp. 147ff.

9/18/90

The now virtually unchallengeable prestige of feminist, Freudian, Marxist criticism and various forms of so-called poststructuralist literary theory associated with the deconstructionism of Jacques Derrida and Paul de Man present an interesting—and perhaps alarming—intellectual puzzle.

The bourgeois ideals of intellectual clarity, the rational and moral probity of the autonomous individual, the organization of civil polity in accordance with positive law instead of tradition and custom, the bureaucratization of life in the service of efficiency and order, the systematic exploitation of the natural world by means of science and technology to "render us the lords and possessors of nature"—this confidence that we could stand as God to ourselves and to the world—is unimaginable apart from its antecedents in the rise of modern physical science out of which emerged not just technology, but also *technique,* the generalization of the attitudes and values of technology to all the modalities of our life in the world.

Technique is an orientation to the nature of things that is possible only when I, in some sense, apprehend myself as enjoying a kind of noetic focus "over here" with the world before and over against me as a coherent totality "over there."

As we have seen, the displacement of the, no doubt, indeterminately situated "subject" amidst the hurly-burly of oral-aural life by the determinate reader before the written, static and—by comparison—"eternal" words of the text made possible, by this transformation of the human sensorium, the first intimation of the revolution that was consummated in the seventeenth century. (May it not indeed be this onset of literacy that produced in hardly more than a generation the shift from the, to us, awkwardly quadrifacial frontality of the "inhumane" sculpture of the so-called Archaic period of Greek art to that we celebrate as the humanism of the Classic period, rather than, as is often suggested, the sudden achievement of new technical skills—as if there could be no question as to what the motivation toward achieving these might have been.)

What is to the point here is the suggestion that the rational complacency of triumphant bourgeois culture in the nineteenth century is rooted in and unintelligible apart from seventeenth century science and technology and the rise of alphabetic chirography and eventually of movable type and printed books.

What has this to do with the new forms of criticism in the academy that, whatever else needs to be said of it, is an attack upon bourgeois culture—frequently terrorist in its tone and tactics? Inasmuch as I have undertaken to show the ways in which, first, literacy and, then, the dualism, useful for the development of science but gratuitously generalized have alienated us from our primitive reality in the world; and inasmuch, too, as feminist, Freudian, Marxist, and deconstructionist criticism, for all their avowed radicalism, in the end found their criticism on the taken-for-granted world of literacy and science. Quite simply, they are not truly radical—their assumption of being so to the contrary notwithstanding.

Each of these forms of criticism in its own way is engaged in exposing the complacency, superficiality, and self-deception of bourgeois life—to say nothing of its profound moral obliquity and suppression of the fact of evil and the tragic sense of life. One of the great ironies in these forms of criticism however is their own superficiality and stupefying aestheticism, more complacent, more removed from seriousness than the worst of their own polemical bêtes noire.

A detailed argument to the claim that none of these is truly radical would require a consideration, case by case, of examples of these forms of criticism. My point is one I wish to make at some remove from such a ringing of the changes: Whatever the merits of their criticisms, whatever may be the light they shed here or there, none grounds its thought in the primordial arché of all meaning and meaning discernment, its mindbody in the world, from which all categories and concepts—including its own—are derived and that are continually retrotended by these. In short, any criticism that would impeach received meanings and values that, by virtue of this oversight of the ground of *all* meaning, not excluding that which is being proffered by the critic, is necessarily a criticism of meaning that is reckless of its own grounds—a criticism *manqué.* This is an intellectually *serious* deficiency only in a form of criticism that presumes to achieve the final exposé, to reach rock bottom, to accomplish an abolition of humankind that in its implicit nihilism takes itself to have affirmed the ultimate value: undeceived honesty. In systematically overlooking the unimpeachable ground of Being in which we are grounded in our lively convivial mindbodies in the world—even the critic in the very act of delivering his critique—criticism with this apocalyptic animus, whatever the half-truths it may avail us, is not incomplete, but disordered.

This is the rock upon which our nihilism—and let us not fail to notice the self-flattery that it conceals—is wrecked.

Is this not what Kierkegaard called "the sickness unto death"—rampant world and self-transcending spirit, at once everywhere and nowhere, alienated from the "power that established it," at one moment plunging into the infinite, in the very next losing itself in the trivial pursuits of narrowness?

And how are we seduced by this? Not by its grandeur, its power of edification, its access to a new way into the nature of things, certainly not its philosophic rigor, which, its arguments hardly ever display.

Are we not ripe for seduction because of the gnostic apocalypticism—the rage to smash this world which is the vile prison of our spirit, fashioned by an evil demiurge and ruled by the servile archons of sexist, racist, class oppression—that is the ambience of the academy? (This observation in no wise tells against the political quest for justice in our political life on each of these matters.) The politicization of the university cannot be understood in political categories. For this we require theological ones.

9/19/90

I am reading again Freud's so-called "Project of 1895," an effort to produce a mechanistic, hydraulic—"Newtonian" (although Helmholz was his mentor in this, it seems)—model of the human psyche. He never quite completed it, he never quite abandoned it—so exigent were the claims upon him of nineteenth century science and the need to justify his enterprise before it. It is a measure of Freud's genius that he could have entertained this absurd aspiration—apparently lifelong—and *still* be able to devise a revolutionary account of human behavior that in no way logically depended upon the mechanistic account of the psyche (though it may have functioned heuristically for Freud as he sought to articulate a metapsychology).

As I read this, to me quite incredible, document, a puzzlement begins to be intimated: *Where is Sigmund Freud?* What is he doing here, talking in this strange way about my psyche, but, even *more* incredibly, about his *own* psyche? How is it possible to do this?

These provoke yet another set of questions on the same "surface" level: Where am I (sitting here, as I am, reading the "Project")? What am I doing with the text, with the hardly even ghostly presence of Freud within its interstices? And how can *this* be done? How can I appropriate the alien, intractable document that is about Freud—the man who actually *wrote* it and wrote in spite of being a "Freudian"; that is, someone who thought quite differently about himself, in terms, for example, of id, ego, super ego, of oedipus complex (after all, an elliptical story), but, even more difficult, about *me,* this person reading this book. (I am aware, even as I rebuke myself for permitting this kind of philosophically irresponsible woolgathering how much it is the Enlightenment in me that reprimands. This speaker in me knows that these are "surface" questions susceptible of "surface" answers; that they are "philosophically trivial" and hence may be philosophically ignored. *Everyone* knows, so it goes, where Freud is, where he or she—the reader—is.)

But the perplexity persists. Where is Sigmund Freud, pen in hand, writing the "Project," carefully choosing each German word (which I see translated in the English text) as it takes its integral place in a communication of its ideas to his friend Wilhelm Fliess? As he shapes each element of his argument to be comprehended by and convincing to its recipient (Freud: "Let's see, how can I be clear, convincing to Fliess? Surely, he will misconstrue my putting it *this* way"), does Freud fantasize *himself* as he writes and *Fliess* as he will read in images drawn from the inertial model of the human mind that he is in the very act of constructing with his written down words; or does his fantasy rather rely upon our mutual common sense, and does he in turn rely upon his fantasy as the very *conditio sine qua non* of his own feat of comprehendingly using his native language as the instrument for the articulation of his thought to another human being? Just to ask these questions is to have them answered. That is why we so readily take them to be philosophically trivial.

For my part, as I reflect upon all this, I find myself before the internally coherent and ingenious model of the "Project," fantasizing the situation of the genius who was its author and who found it convincing. This juxtaposition of the model and my fantasy renders the model utterly incredible. For the model of the "Project" clearly cannot be integrated by a set of *explicit* rules to the terms in which I am just now aware of myself. There is no way to get from it to them without leaping an enormous logical gap. Nor can the repertoire of quasi-mechanistic concepts of which the model is composed be translated by any set of *explicit* transformation rules into the images of my fantasy of Freud and Fliess, reading, talking, reflecting, by means of which I try to make the missing men present to this account of mind.

Clearly, Freud continued to consider the "Project" and its model deserving of his attention, notwithstanding the lack of any commensurability between it and what we know from other sources was his own sense of himself. If he does not notice this incommensurability, then it can only be because there are tacit acts of intellection and judgment at work on Freud's part (and on my part), rescuing *mere* explicit thought from bankruptcy. What cannot be made to hold together as the heterogeneous features—the inertial model of 1895 and common sense—of a complete, integral, and articulated model of the human mind, *can* be held together and endowed with the potency to do its heuristic work in the lively mindbody of Sigmund Freud, relying upon his inarticulate, indeed, inarticulable powers to achieve an integration.

Yet it is just *this* Freud who is absent from Freud's own text. It is the Freud that is suppressed, the Freud that is systematically kept out of sight, the *mindbodily* Freud that is primitive, more fundamental, possessing superordinate and unimpeachable authority, that always remains at his back because of literacy's inherent tendency to reduce our immediate, commonsense feel for the world.

The author of spoken words in an oral-aural colloquy is after all vividly reminded of the concrete reality in the ordinary world of oneself and one's co–colloquists.

In writing a text, unless it is a personal letter, the author addresses his or her abstract language—the language, that is to say, defined by a "subject matter" addressed to whomsoever it may concern, to no one in particular. The concrete reality in the ordinary world of neither the reader nor the writer can make an explicit appearance in the text.

The text however can make sense only when the author as he writes and the reader as she reads tacitly supply the concrete stage setting within which they actually dwell as they are writing and reading and that bring the abstractions to ground.

Freud was there all along, writing away on the "Project of 1895"; and I, William Poteat, was there as well, making sense of what, taken in itself, is quite absurd by placing it in a context in which its absurdity is mitigated in order that it may do its heuristic work.

We can understand an exhaustively neurophysiological model of the human mind only because we tacitly *refuse to accept it* as exhaustive. We exegete the model by "reading" it in the context of ordinary human consciousness and the things we say to one another in everyday discourse about what we think, feel, and have noticed about the world around us. If we did not, the neurophysiological model would make absolutely no sense. To apprehend and evaluate the logic of the model requires its appraisal by a mind not itself reducible to it. Its "internal" logic is parasitical upon reference to an "external" sentient, oriented, and motile human being existing in the world.

9/20/90

Yet, if Freud found this "Newtonian" model of the psyche plausible or heuristically powerful, it is because, in spite of all, he brings, cannot help bringing, himself, his lively sentient, motile, and oriented mindbody, with all its inarticulate complexity to this otherwise bare and putatively totally explicit text of the "Project." And if I find the model in the text plausible or useful—or just worth my passing attention—it is because I tacitly import into my understanding the Freud I know from his biography, from his *Interpretation of Dreams,* from his case studies of patients, and so forth, in short, a man, though possessed of genius and daring, is yet like myself, vainglorious, unforgiving, jealous, worried about paying his bills, going about his quotidian life perceiving himself and being perceived in the midst of these affairs in the most ordinary but incredibly rich ways of our common sense, owing nothing to the model of the "Project of 1895" and very little to the lexicon of a psychoanalytic metapsychology; it is because, I say, I place the "Project" in this context—a context that also includes me and my mindbody, its logical powers surreptitiously supplying sense tacitly where it does not and could not exists with the putatively total explicitness of the model in the text of the "Project," *taken by itself.*

A metapsychology is the work of someone reflecting from out of his or her mindbody upon the nature of "mind." Reflexivity is "mind's" ultimate power—or so at any rate we, in a literate culture, take for granted—yet it is precisely this—reflexivity itself—that, as it may make all other sorts of things its objects, systematically eludes itself, in an infinite regress. (How *could* this be *strictly* true? I should not be able to say so, if it were.) So long as reflection from out of our mindbodies seeks itself as an object among objects, it will fail to find itself. Yet, because it can never lose itself, it tacitly demands and fashions a sense of, a way of appropriating, even models of itself that in its absence would strike one as obviously absurd.

Criticism, whether it be feminist, Marxist, Freudian, deconstructive, or what not, can hardly fail to commit what Whitehead called "the fallacy of misplaced concreteness," which he imputed in particular to *scientism*—that general "philosophical" view that intellectuals, who were a laity to the actual practice of natural science, inferred, not without encouragement from early scientists themselves. This "philosophy" took the seventeenth century's necessarily *abstract account* of the nature of physical things to be the *nature* of things themselves, the *actual,* that is, the actually *existent;* in short, the nature of things in the concrete. For the actual, concrete world in which each of us finds him-or herself to be the most concrete, that is, densest, entity there is, scientism substituted the *abstract account* of the nature of things given in physics and chemistry and by implication claimed that this was the *real* world, indeed, the world in which we *really* live.

Criticism as we understand and practice it is, as we have seen, a progeny of alphabetic literacy. Obviously it is far easier to perform a critique upon a written text of a given length than upon a viva voce disquisition of roughly the same number of words. In the first case one has before one a permanent document to which one can refer repeatedly and at one's own pace. In the case even of a modest library one has a whole and permanent "world" all the particulars of which are *virtually* simultaneously present. The forward surge of time, periodized by the reciprocity of speaking, hearing, answering of orality begins to become a disvalue.

The impact upon the human imagination of the picture of a whole world embodied in words, its parts simultaneously present as in a library, gave rise to the concept of a world-view and criticism as *we* now understand and practice it. Criticism is possible when there is before us a stable object upon which we can have a *perspective* and can therefore describe and evaluate as a whole.

The magic of written or printed *words*—words that can be seen—has given us this enormous new power and control. Is there any wonder then that *articulation*—*words* that can be revisited indefinitely—should acquire a new value in the hierarchy of the human sensorium? Is there any wonder that compared to the value of written and therefore *permanent articulation* all the modes of our inarticulate being, especially the unarticulated logos that informs our mindbodily existence begins to decline in value? Is it a surprise that *word* now becomes more and more paragimatically the *written* word and the *written* word becomes—never mind its abstractness—the paradigm of reality; that *thought* is embodiment in *words, explicitation, reflection,* not the vanishing word of oral-aural reciprocity, even less the mindbodily gestural ambience of those embodiments of meaning and logos in time, but articulation in vectors that, even though they at the moment lack the permanence of the printed word, are imagined to be capable of and have their true consummation in a written text? Is not the slide into the "fallacy of misplaced concreteness" precisely what, given all this, we should expect?

9/21/90

In placing a *reader* in a determinate location in visual space before a static, "finite" (in the sense of being capable in principle of appearing as a determinate, simultaneously present totality), and visible text, the images of literacy predisposed our imaginations toward stasis and determinacy (of more or less sharpness of focus) as the superordinate features of the world we henceforth took ourselves to be in.

With a "visually" lucid object on one side and a determinate subject in an identifiable locus on the other, the *penumbra* that surrounds every lucent object in our awareness of the actual world is sytematically eliminated. When *thought as such* is identified with its *embodiment in words,* with articulation, awareness tends to be identified with the lucid center of consciousness.

In this economy of the imagination wrought by print, even if we necessarily fail at trying to make the world and ourselves in it into a lucid spectacle, it was nevertheless toward this that we were to aspire.

Literacy obscures, not to say eliminates, the ground of all meaning and meaning-discernment that our sentient, motile, and oriented mindbodies precisely are, from which all these reflective enterprises derive and that has its appearance at our backs, in the penumbra. No less do the images of literacy, the better to focus upon its determinate object, abstract what it takes to be the paradigmatically real from its *actual* context in the great world. (Surely we cannot imagine the emergence of Renaissance linear perspective apart from the advancing habituation of Europeans to the printed word and its values; even as we can best appreciate Cézanne's great assault upon this perspective as the effort to paint the penumbra back into the visual representation of the world and humankind's "place" in it. Indeed, to behold and in beholding to be beheld by a landscape of Cézanne is to recover something of the penumbra of one's own mindbody.)

None of these remarks constitutes any sort of impeachment, as such, of criticism as we have practiced it—as if we had any choice—nor does it call into question the heuristic potency and edification available through particular instances of it.

What is implied in this phenomenological analysis is that criticism such as is practiced among us literate types is defined by limits that are heavy with epistemological and ontological imports; limits that, whatever the powers with which they have endowed us, no less have mortified our being. No one ever has or could live and move and have his or her being in the world that, product of misplaced concreteness that it is, is presented to us in criticism.

The criticism that emerges with literacy is, then,

first of all, *abstract:* abstract because of the assimilation of *thought as such* to embodiment in words; because it is *an* abstract—as all *language* is an abstract, an epitome, an abridgment of the world in its actuality, the written word more so than the spoken. This being so, what has been epitomized has been decontextualized.

Criticism is also driven toward *ecumenism,* the desire for totality, to "see" the world that is its object as a "finite" whole upon which its categories and concepts—'primitive communism,' 'means and modes of production,' 'false consciousness,' 'scientific socialism,' 'dialectical materialism,' and so on, or 'id,' 'ego,' 'superego,' 'repressed material,' 'oedipal complex,' 'neurosis,' and the rest—can achieve closure.

A third characteristic of criticism, closely connected with the second, is what I shall call *ontological monism,* the, perhaps natural, tendency to take the decontextualized "world" that is the fruit of one's criticism to be the *only* or the only *important, real, valuable* world there is and to take the categories and concepts that embody that "world" to be the *only* or the only *important, real, valuable* categories and concepts for apprehending the world—everything at bottom, or *seriously,* is Marxism or Freudianism or feminism. (Of course no one ever *explicitly* makes this claim. It is so deeply buried in the history of our practice that we never notice it. This is the source of its power over us. And when it is hinted at, it often provokes outrage.) This monism (are not all monisms?) is naturally reductionistic—as is *all* reflection that is a child of this literacy.

But is not monism our precarious hedge against the chaos of an infinite plurality? The pluralistic "elements" of the world in which we actually live and move and have our being achieve their integration through the pretensions toward "rational" coherence that are natural to the lively mindbodies of each of us and all of us together—both prior to and issuing in reflection.

If number has a meaning for you only in the highly parochial practice of counting concrete objects—say, numbering things on fingers and toes—you are not likely to infer Pythagoreanism from the offhand discovery that the tone sounded by the vibrations of a string is a function of the string's length. But empowered by a written language, thereby moved toward abstraction, ecumenism, and monism, you will, in due course, be led to conclude from your discovery about the string that the nature of *absolutely everything* can be understood only as a function of numerical ratios, as with Pythagoreanism. Put this with some other premises and soon you have physical science and then you get that all but unassailable derangement of the modern mind wrought by abstraction, ecumenism, and monism, namely, scientism.

•

9/24/90

The world we are given in the metapsychology in the corpus of Freud's writings—for all its discovery of the dark places in the human soul that were either forgotten or previously unknown; for all its exposure of the dynamics of self-deception, the unforgettable fact in each our lives of having been born of woman by man, in a state of dependency and terror; for all of the fact that Freud, "to us . . . no more a person / now but a whole climate of opinion . . ."[q]—is too narrow, abstract, mortified a world

[q]W. H. Auden, "In Memory of Sigmund Freud."

for us to live in. Even Auden's elegy for Freud, rich with allusions to the "shades that still waited to enter / The bright circle of his recognition . . ." is a world that answers more fully to our complex demand for meaning than the whole of the Freudian psychology, *taken strictly by itself*. And of course, Freud would agree. It was he, after all who said, when asked for the meaning of a large cigar he had lighted up at the conclusion of a paper he had read to a gathering of psychologists: "There are times when a good cigar is nothing but a good cigar"—in saying which he paid tribute to the "overdetermination" of the human situation, to the *authority* of our commonsense dealings with one another.

A graduate student of mine some years ago brought this home to me with both force and poignancy. An Armenian, educated in Lebanon and at the Harvard Medical School, certified by the profession as a psychoanalyst, and more recently, having completed his degree in Divinity, he was undertaking to earn the Ph.D in Religion.

It was our convenience for me to meet him in his physician's office every Wednesday afternoon for us to cover some material of mutual interest under the rubric of "Independent Study for Graduate Students."

As our project wound toward its conclusion—we were investigating the epistemological credentials of Freud's metapsychology—I asked him one afternoon: "How, John, can you reconcile your adherence to orthodox Freudian theory and practice with your beliefs as a Christian?" "Let me show you a picture," he said, drawing my attention to an aged 6 × 10 black and white photograph, framed and hanging on the wall. There were eight adults in the picture, obviously of the same generation, men and women, garbed in the native dress of Armenian's living in Aleppo in the early 1920s.

"The patriarchal figure standing in the middle of the group is my grandfather. All the others are his siblings, my great aunts and uncles.

"Sometime during the period 1914–18, the Turks began systematically to massacre the Armenian population. They were marched down to the Euphrates River and hacked to pieces, their arms and legs, heads and torsos tossed into the river.

My grandfather, alerted to the impending disaster, had sewn pieces of gold into his long coat. As he was herded by the soldiers with his brothers and sisters, for whom, as the oldest son he was responsible, toward their terrible destiny, under the cover of night he bribed first one soldier and then another, to release into the darkness members of his family, one by one.

"Here, the survivors are gathered together in a garden in Aleppo for a picnic on a Sunday afternoon, perhaps ten years after their ordeal.

"All this happened before I was born, yet here I am. What is the point? The point is that what Freudian metapsychology can say, in its own strictly observed limits, about the heights and depths of human reality in the world, brought from the lives and histories of the people into the rich texture and concentration of this photograph in that time and place is—valuable as it is for cultural analysis, even more valuable as it may be as psychoanalytic therapy—next to nothing. The lives and histories, their meaning to themselves and to one another, the meaning for the world of just these eight people are too complex and rich to be understood, to be participated in in terms of Freudian categories alone."

Great intellectual innovators such as Marx and Freud are rarely as rigid in their application of their insights as are their followers. Intellectual restlessness tends to be their stock in trade.

The rest of us however, under the suasions of values and images we have introjected from alphabetic literacy that have hardened the way in which we practice criticism into the *abstraction* of identifying thought as such with its embodiment in language, the *ecumenism* that gravitates toward seeing its object as a finite totality, and the drift toward *ontological monism* that tends to decontextualize its object, are seduced into critical absolutisms of one sort or another.

We hardly ever make this explicit claim about the significance of our criticism. If *asked* to do so, most of us would indignantly refuse.

The gravitational pull in these directions is, however, as old as the writing and reading of words. *This* is the source of our new power and of our alienation from our own ground. It is a habit that is two and a half millenia old. It underlies the usually unrecognized drift toward reductionism that has become more powerful since the seventeenth century.

When criticism as abstraction, ecumenism, and monism is joined, as it has been in the academy, by the equally powerful motif in our sensibility of a world-transcending spiritual denial of the world, of a will to destroy what is given to free ourselves from the bondage of this creature of an evil demiurge—when, in short, criticism becomes gnostic apocalypticism—our self-destruction is well-nigh complete.

When our criticism thus became *explicitly* reductive, when that is, its raison d'être began to be the wholesale replacement of the literary text with, first, a new and preferred reality and, eventually, with the doctrine of the undecidability of the meaning of signs, with the consequent disappearance of reality itself, nihilism was triumphant. Only a deadly form of aestheticism, a growing loss of the power to be *serious* can make these catastrophes seem like clever games rather than nightmare.

Shame on me for *my* apocalypticism!

9/25/90

In an essay attributed to a certain Author A that Kierkegaard claims to have found in an antique secretary that he had purchased and that is entitled "The Immediate Erotic Stages or The Musical-Erotic," the author, in showing that Mozart's opera *Don Giovanni* is the greatest work of art ever produced, introduces the distinctions abstract idea–concrete idea, abstract medium–concrete medium. In the opera, according to A, there is the unique perfect marriage of its idea, eroticism, and its medium, music.

Little attention has been given to this essay. It is by turns ironical, romantic, always aesthetical, at times rather precious, and of course pseudonymous, therefore perhaps to be attended to only as a part of S. K.'s overall stratagem and not taken seriously as in itself an exercise in phenomenology.

And there were always Hegel's "Lectures on Aesthetics" under whose aegis A's essay was alleged to have been written. The ideas of the "Musical Erotic" could therefore be seen to be not Kierkegaard's because they were Author A's and not Author A's because they were Hegel's.

These scholarly minuets make it possible for us to

ignore the possibly important question: Never mind the role being played by Author A in the Kierkegaardian chess game, what is he talking about? (A strong case could be made for the claim that this essay and that other piece by the same hand, "The Ancient Tragical Motif," taken together, are the profoundest analysis of modern Western culture that we have. I will make the claim, but defer the making of the strong case until another time.)

What does Author A in his argument mean by *idea* and *medium?* Let me suggest the following.

An idea—here we must abandon all our intellectual habits—is the particular form, shape, resonance, thrust, texture, orientation, tonality, rhythm, intentionality, affective sound, and coloration of the world formed in the conjunction of my hitherto undifferentiated being (my primitive mindbodily being is, in its primordial ordinations, *differentiated* antecedent to its "differentiation") and a particular medium (etymologically, as I have observed earlier, a medium is something that cuts asunder, interrupts, intervenes upon something else that possesses some form of wholeness, integrity, coherence; but as medium, that which sunders, it is at the same time a mediator referring the sundered parts to one another, doing the work of mediation, acting as a go-between—a medium as go-between acquires the sense of a vector, the embodiment of, the bearer of meaning) that is the vector of this differentiation. Idea is that mode of being-in-the-world that I both have and am in the midst of as the result of my appearing through a given medium. It is that structure through and within which I appear in the world; it is the shape of the being that I both am and have when I am projected by some particular medium from out of the background of immediacy upon a particular "otherness" vis-à-vis myself.

When the medium by which immediacy is ruptured is abstract—that is, tending to draw me away from that density that is the center of things which is myself—I shall appear in the world abstractly—as does Don Giovanni, who exists *only* in the music of the opera; as I do, as I give into Don Giovanni's solely musical existence (I would need to shed that density at the center of things that I am to exist as Don Giovanni does). When the medium is concrete, that is, tending to draw me back to that density at the center of things that I am, I shall be in the world concretely.

What is the most *concrete* medium? The one in which reference can be made to the densest of all entities, namely, that in the world that is reflexively named by *here, now,* and *I.* Only language possesses the means for doing this. What is the most *abstract* medium? That which draws me away from *here, now, I.*

Architecture, sculpture, and painting, by reason of their relative stasis, their being in time statically, the time of endurance, and therefore by addressing themselves to me in my co-presence in space with myself and with these media, do not draw me away in the dynamic time of music from *here, now,* and *I.* Music in *its* time "hurries in a perpetual vanishing."

My mode of being in the world, *whatever* it may be, is always mediated through particular media. I may therefore say that a medium is my existential dwelling place for as long as it informs my being. The mode of my existence, in other words, is shaped by the idea that is given in the fracturing of my hitherto unmediated being by the opposing to it of a particular medium. Obviously in the course of any given day, hour, or moment my mode of being is alternately, indeed, usually simultaneously, hence dissonantly, informed by and mediated through many different media; hence in the course of these times my mode of being embodies many different ideas.

Let us take an example from architecture and sculpture. It might be said: Sculpture is existential mass exhaustively filling space; whereas architecture is the ordering of empty space by means of the organization of masses. In a limited sense this is true. Obviously, the "negative" spaces of architecture—the emptiness, both internal and external—are on a scale and of a design to permit the deployment of human bodies within them for the performance of certain activities; whereas this is generally not the case with sculpture.

But this is to ignore the way in which sculpture in fact also organizes masses, *thereby* ordering the emptinesses that environ it, no less than the emptinesses within it; for example, the sculpture of Henry Moore.

The disanalogies between sculpture and architecture are real, but perhaps not so important phenomenologically as the analogies between them—at least, so far as Author A's inquiry goes.

9/26/90

Any mass, architectural or sculptural, orders the emptiness both within it and around it.

What does it mean to say this? The given architecture or sculpture has a form (is a physical mass) in a scale (in relation to the paradigmatic mass and scale of my body in the world) which forms the mise-en-scène of my being-in-the-world. According to its form and scale it will overwhelm, uplift, protect, enclose, cramp, or enlarge the world in which I dwell when present to it. Michaelangelo's *David* structures its environing space according to its form, its scale (in relation to my body), its location, its situation vis-à-vis my body, its "motility," its humanity (as I conceive this), its vitality; and it is the other side, as it is also the medium of, the particular way that *I,* at that moment, dwell in and appreciate my own mindbodily being-in-the-world. This phenomenon—my dwelling in the world in a certain way through the mediation of sculpture—is not something derived, second order, merely "psychological." It is radical, bed rock, ontological—antecedent to the distinctions mind-body, psyche-soma, and so forth. This is a description of one of the ways that I am in the world in the most primitive sense.

When Author A, then, speaks of an idea, we must take *idea* to refer to the mode of being-in-the-world, the ontologically radical ambience, that is induced for us by a certain medium that mediates a world—shapes an idea by introducing oppugnancy in the midst of immediacy. An idea, that is, a mode of being-in-the-world, is *concrete* when it is one in which, by reason of its retrotension of that density at the center of the world that is myself and is thus close to the springs of my action—action as speech, as appearance *in* speech—is natural and intrinsic to it (architecture from this point of view is a concrete medium since, often, it induces a surrounding where worship, speech, a space of appearance—where speech can be uttered and taken up—are natural and intrinsic); whereas an idea, that is, a mode of being-in-the-world, is *abstract* when it draws me away from that density that is my self at the center of things and therefore is one to which action as appearance in speech is not so natural and intrinsic. Grandeur and motility are natural to the *umvelt* induced by *David*—as perhaps neither is to that induced by the sixth century *kouroi*—that give us a mise-en-scène in which by comparison we are cramped, crabbed, immobile. Don Giovanni whose medium is music, whose idea, that is, whose world, is therefore the musical erotic, of course, never speaks. In his world, his existence-sphere, there is no room for speech, only the elemental sound of passion, existing in a perpetual vanishing.

Music, eroticism, and madness—since the appearance of the blaspheming "El Burlador de Sevilla" this seems to have been the destiny of the Western world.

5/25/92

As we have seen, the alliance in the reflected, second-order account of the nature of things in a culture dominated by the values and imaginative infrastructure of literacy ensures and ubiquitously reenforces a deep-seated and well-nigh inseparable conceptual bond between being *real* and being *stabile.* In such an ethos the role in the articulation of the world of putatively fugitive memory and inconstant and promiscuous imagination are taken to be peculiarly problematic.

When however these are apprehended from within the convivial, mindbodily matrix of our ordinary doings and sayings, will their natures and roles appear to be different?

In short, can "Imagination [be] redeemed from promiscuous fornication with her own images?" (W. H. Auden).

The distinction between logos and mythos that hardened as a literate culture began to take the place of orality became by the seventeenth century what Whitehead called "the bifurcation of nature"; nature as it is eternally in itself and nature as it is apprehended by us and, alas, so the thought was, adorned, festooned—and falsified—by the secondary qualities supplied by our senses.

Though in the event it required centuries to become the heteronomy with which we now live on such cozy terms as to be the fate we have come to love, what in fact happened over more than two millennia, was, at a stroke, proleptically to render problematic *for reflection* whole tracts of the ordinary world in which we actually live and die, where these tracts are not at all suspect, where indeed as *discriminated tracts* they do not even *exist,* where the "myth" of a Last Judgement bears heavier *ontological* weight for our existence between birth and death than the general theory of relativity—one of which, in this bifurcation, is taken not to be about reality, the other of which is.

The form of the opposition between logos and mythos—whatever the changing nomenclature—has varied greatly over the course of its history. But it is not too much to say that with Plato's banishment of the poets from his ideal republic, in reflection, the role of imagination in human sensibility came to be authorized only by such analogies as it was perceived to have with logos and by its complementation of the latter's powers.

Logos evolved into the lean rationality that was consonant with the apprehension of the primary qualities of things—length, breadth, depth, velocity of motion; in short, grasped reality as it eternally is, apart from its being known by us. Whereas mythos came to be seen as the inconstant, delusory, and elusively dynamic world of our senses; in short, it became *imagination* in the now ontologically and epistemologically pejorative sense. And usually both thinking and imagining were pictured *essentially* as activities of a discarnate mind with, at most, an equivocal connection to our flesh.

5/26/92

Remembering and imagining, archaically implicated with one another, are radical intentions of my sentient, oriented, motile mindbody in the world. Imagination, assisted by memory, pretensively calls forth the world and ourselves, at once *in* the world and *over against it,* from the background of the indeterminate other in figures of our own devising; memory assisted by imagination, retrotensively marks, disposes, and funds our engagements with the "things" and "events" of the world that thus stand forth.

The sense that written and then printed words were not only permanent by comparison with the fugitive words we actually speak, but even with the public recitations of the Greek epics by rhapsodes, who, by their reiteration of repeated formulae and tropes, gave a permanence and transmissibility to the stories not possessed by our casual speech was a powerful seduction for human sensibility. Not only was writing clearly superior to the oral-aural word for the achievement of a wide range of practical goals. This practical superiority of permanent writing to evanescent speech, endowing us with an hitherto unimaginable power, naturally led to the sense that the practically permanent, static (as compared with the viva voce spoken word), eternal, finite (as the possible combinations and permutations of the letters of the Greek alphabet are finite in number), and in time, to the belief that the practical power of the written word is an earnest of its being the definitive model of and hence access to the real that was, like written words themselves, eternal, finite, and static.

This was the ultimate setting within which meaning and intelligibility paradigmatically appeared, alienated from the reciprocity of human speaking and hearing, where intellection was fulfilled by performing and apprehending acts of living speech to—in the Platonic case—an eternal realm of logoi.

Reality is henceforth abstracted from the temporal surge and flow of the oral-aural reciprocity of our quotidian life, even as written and printed words are. Meaning and intelligibility, alienated to an unchanging realm, are no longer grounded in the dynamism of our convivial, sentient, oriented, intentional mindbodies that are their true provenance and continuing authorization.

5/27/92

No solution lies in the direction of simply standing the hierarchy, primary qualities–secondary qualities, on its head. Nothing would be changed. After all, it is not too outrageous to suggest that there are analogies among the oppositions posited between primary qualities–secondary qualities, literacy values–orality values, and one form or another of philosophical realism–philosophical idealism: the first terms in each of these pairs exhibit a nisus toward abstraction from the world in which we live and move and have our being; the second terms tend to draw us back into the concrete setting of ordinary life.

Our failure to define a dynamic matrix of all meaning and meaning discernment, to disclose an incessant nisus toward a lively comprehension and integration of both terms in these dualisms, suggests that the original framing of our reflected account of the world is faulty. It can be shown—as I shall do—that, for example, so-called primary qualities and secondary qualities are in fact ontologically connate, their common provenance being our lively, intentional, sentient, oriented, and convivial mindbodies in the world, at once antecedent to and the source of reflected logos.

Rather than making yet another 180° turn on the fixed axis around which the thought of some 2500 years has turned, we shall have to remove to a radically new one, namely, to the logos that ubiquitously enforms our unreflected intentional and convivial mindbodies and that issues in the reflection borne by figures of its own devising, in science, philosophy—indeed, in the whole of culture's usages and artifacts.

Only so can we display the truth about imagination, memory, and culture that has been obscured by the superordination of the permanent and static written (and eventually the printed) word as paradigmatic embodiment of meaning and logos over the dynamic and fugitive spoken word of the oral-aural reciprocity.

My mindbody as imagination—as, that is, the pretension toward order, meaning, coherence, closure, logos—devises, that is, defines and arrests, an articulation within the hitherto indeterminate. This can be a wonted rhythmical movement obedient to a tropism, a repertoire of gestures, a tone of voice, a style, cadence, and pace of speech, a manner of bearing my erect body in opposition to the pull of gravity, the ordinations *of* time and space and *in* time and space of my lively and expressive mindbody, my ordered motility and style of walk, my rhythmical breathing, my song and dance, my ritual movement in agreement with the cadence of the earth in its diurnal-nocturnal course, my civil reenactment of our story.

In time and through habituation, what Merleau-Ponty calls *sedimentation,* these and untold others become *usages:* what and the way in which we do and say;

what and the way in which we are given to doing and saying; the repertoire of instruments and gestures that are their means—words and concepts, by what they exclude and what they include, establish one existential environment rather than some other, the pace and mode of our travel, the rhythms and horizons of our technology, the music, sculpture, architecture that, by forming spaces in which we dwell, will frame the spatiality of our mindbodily self-apprehensions.

All these together—and of course much else as well—constitute, to gloss a Wittgensteinian phrase, the form of our life. Our mindbodies as imagination in its pretension toward meaning and coherence shapes and articulates the world and ourselves in it.

Such usages assert themselves as crossing points of our mindbodies with the world, thereby through their offices appointing each as over against the other in a certain way rather than in some other.

Through the foregoing I have sought to grasp *in* reflection that which is itself the radix and provenance *of* reflexion, namely, the primordial relations between my mindbody and its—our—dynamic world. This I have undertaken to do in language that will bear the marks of its rootedness in the prehistory and history of my mindbody that I apprehend without mediation as the intentional background and arché of all meaning and meaning discernment; the mindbody that pretends and through imagination, in a sense, forms an emerging reality over against itself, that reality in turn retrotends.

5/28/92

Obviously in our quotidian comings and goings, doings and sayings we may be said at a given moment, however unreflectingly, to appreciate and to act upon the assumption that there are boundaries between "ourselves" and the "world," even if they are dynamic and mutable, and even if they are "defined," at a given moment, by the activity in which we are then engaged.

On its face this appears to be a rather fastidious way of referring to what we are likely to believe is the *commonsense* problem of the "self and the other." There *is* however no "commonsense" problem of the self and the other. In the course of pursuing our ordinary affairs—unless our ordinary affairs are exhaustively consumed by teaching, reading, and writing philosophy—we hardly ever make a reference to "the relations between the self and the other"; our ordinary activities hardly ever depend upon our doing so.

The "problem of the self and the other" is, in other words, an invention of philosophers. The particular way in which the "self" and the "world" have been conceived in themselves and the view of the nature of their opposition to one another has, in the Western philosophic tradition, issued in notorious and crippling dualisms.

If however, fastidious or not, the objective of this inquiry is precisely to find a new kind of discourse that can show forth the derivation of even the most abstract and rarified concepts of our *wissenschaftlich* intellection from the logos that enforms our as-yet-unreflected mind-bodily sentience, orientation, and motility, anterior to duality, then we shall have to transfer the colloquy holus-bolus to a radically new axis point. This will mean that we can no longer uncritically assume that the speech of our ordinary doings and sayings—of what we think of as philosophically neutral common sense—is impermeable to the concepts of our inherited philosophic dualisms. Quite the contrary. And *this* means that we will have to undertake the arduous, not to say at times harrowing, labor of devising as we go a new rhetoric that consciously eschews the dualistic metaphors and implications built into our putatively philosophically neutral ordinary language and that ransacks our language—even its etymology—for words and forms wherein the built-in metaphors and their implications, even if they are not always unequivocally monistic in import, will, in the novelty of their juxtaposition to our occasionally tainted ordinary language, reveal the dualism often found even there.

There is no implication in this that the language of self-other, subject-object, and other dual distinctions in either theoretical or commonsensical usages are illicit. The case is rather that they are vectors *of our own devising*—reflective instruments fashioned by us out of the coitus between our mindbodies and the world that through them achieves articulation to serve some theoretical or practical telos and that they are derived from and always remain rooted in the dynamic coherence continually being fashioned by our radical mindbodies, which even so is always in danger of being sundered by abstraction into static dualisms.

Whatever dual—or other—distinctions we may in our human autonomy devise as vectors of reflection, they can never exist *over against* us as heteronomies, as the *object* is thought, according to the regnant view, to be heteronomously opposed to ourselves as subjects, according to the regnant view.

5/29/92

There is then a pretensive-retrotensive cadence to the life of my mindbody in the world. My being is intentional through and through from its most primitive operative ordinations, far below the level of ordinary awareness and conscious control—no less disposed on that account, however, toward the arché of all value and coherence—to my most delicate and cultivated feats of pneunocarnal coordination, from my mindbodily appropriation of the world's as yet mute axioms of significance to my entry into the logos of Gödel's Incompleteness Theorem and J. S. Bach's *The Art of the Fugue.* Thus I am a creature of time, memory, and imagination. *Memory* and *imagination* identify two of the modes in which the intentionality of my mindbody unfolds in the world.[r]

If this were not so, I could not even apprehend my own heart beat as a *beat.* Consider this.

If the imagination, lying beyond my power to exert my will upon it and usually beneath the level of my ordinary awareness, could not in one moment reach forward toward a closure of an intimation of coherence and meaning and memory, subject to the same strictures, could not simultaneously bring forward a mindbodily memory of the previous moment and the "beat" that it contained, I could not apprehend my heart as beating. At this remove from ordinary awareness it is my *flesh* that imagines; my *flesh* that remembers—not "flesh" as this is mediated through the categories of gross anatomy, physiology, mo-

---

[r]Indeed, *one* of the ways to characterize my mindbody as being intentional from "top to bottom," as being sentient, oriented, and motile, is to say that it is enformed through and through in the very tonus of my flesh by the pretensions of imagination and retrotensions of memory. Imagination and memory are therefore not faculties I exercise; they are among the conditions of my existence.

lecular biology, but flesh as this appears unmediated in the tonality of my living mindbody.

The gestalt that I hear or feel in reflection as a *beat,* as, that is, a pretension of imagination and a retrotension of memory, is laid down in the most primitive intentionalities of my mindbody, far beyond the reach of reflection, yet apprehended in the very grain and texture of its being alive in time. If there were no such pretension of imagination and no such retrotension of memory *in my flesh,* then, quite simply, there could *be* no beat; hence a fortiori there could be no knowledge of one.

This appeal to a *mindbodily* memory and imagination that quicken and entone the entire hierarchy of the modes of our sentience and orientation is to be understood as *logically heterogeneous* in relation to any appeal that might be made to the neurophysiology of the *central nervous system.* The latter is of course authoritative as a topography of certain of our physical characteristics, and a theory as to the functioning of the neurophysiological system such that anomalies in our ordinary behavior can be shown to be related to anomalies in the system.

The discourse in which this theory is formulated is severely, and quite properly, limited. It is *incomplete* inasmuch as a neurophysiological system is "blind" and cannot stand on its own. It requires—*conceptually*—an embodiment in a living (sentient and oriented) organism just to be recognized for what it is. To speak of the central nervous system as performing this or that feat for a living organism oriented in the world is surreptitiously to introduce concepts that strictly have no place in the conceptual repertoire of neurology. Yet it is just this move that endows the neurophysiological model with a sense it otherwise lacks. A neuroelectric event neither remembers nor forgets: it fires or it does not fire.

My lively, sentient, oriented, and motile *mindbody,* ontologically and epistemologically prior to (and, indeed, the very source of) the science of neurophysiology, performs its incarnate feats of remembering and imagining. *I,* environed by the ordinary world, remember; *I* imagine. Usually I can apprehend my heartbeat by placing a finger on my carotid artery. Sometimes when I have exerted myself strenuously I can feel it beating in my chest.

In both of these cases I am apprehending a gestalt that is the work of the mindbody's incarnate memory and imagination beneath the level of ordinary awareness. The explicit knowledge of my heart beat that I have in reflection abides first in the unreflected logos of my intentional mindbody upon which both its *being* and its *being known* equally depend even if differently. Even with my heartbeat electronically amplified for my ears and depicted for my eyes as a pulsing line moving across a computer screen, if my beating heart, creature that it is of the primordial imagination and memory of my flesh, were not communicated through every stratum of my lively being, the matrix for an apprehension of even the sonic and the visual beat would not exist; I should be quite deaf and blind to it.

Thus even our highest intellectual powers derive from and never cease to depend upon this ground of all meaning and meaning discernment: our tonic, intentional, sentient, and oriented mindbodies in the world that cannot lucently appear before reflection and yet show themselves ubiquitously in our experience of being alive.

Our language has the sinews of our bodies that had them first. Its grammar, syntax, metaphorical and semantical intentionalities were first and are still the "grammar," "syntax," "metaphorical" and "semantical intentionalities" of our mindbodies.

Far, then, from being faculties of our minds *simpliciter,* memory and imagination are at the very heart of our intentional being in the world, prior to all articulate duality. Memory and imagination are two ways in which our mindbodies have of directing themselves at the world that they themselves have caused to stand forth from the indeterminate other.

My whole mindbody, then, participates in my every act of "imagining" and "remembering," sensing and moving, knowing and thinking, judging and speaking—whether reflected or as yet far removed from reflection. The same logos of my mindbody in which inhere all meaning and meaning discernment and that both *forms* and *is expressed* in the beating heart of my living flesh issues in the coherence of my speech with my gestures, in my physical and psychological equilibrium, in my participation in the prelingual meaning of the native language I see and hear spoken around me before I have "acquired" that language (and as the condition of my doing so); it issues as well in Gödel's theorem and in the comprehension of it, in Bach's *Suites for Unaccompanied Cello* and my "hearing" of them, in Kant's *Critique of Pure Reason* and Kierkegaard's *Either/Or* and in my exegesis of them; and of course it has issued in the sum of the words I have here drawn out of my mindbody and written on the previous pages, and in my comprehension of them and in my offering of them to your comprehension.

6/1/92

Let us look at this from a different angle.

As I write I continually revisit reflexively what I

have said and written, not so much to remark its semantic substance as to be reminded of the *ontological weight* of my own words as unique and inexchangeable marks of my *being* that shows itself in the agonistic search among the linguistic and extralinguistic resources husbanded in the history and present reality of my intentional mindbody and in the power that, in utterance, has made them actual.

Digging the words out of the prelinguistic ground that is my mindbody in the world, allowing the *words* at length to surface, is the actualization of speech—assertion—that is the paradigmatic action by which *I am*.

My entanglement in this turbid transaction between me and the forming of my spoken and written words—so conceived—that authorizes my claim that that logos manifest in our so-called higher powers of reflective intellection retrotends the logos that orders the life and action of our mindbodies even in their most primitive forms of sentience and orientation.

Words on my tongue and lips at the brink of an entry into the space of appearance have derived from and still depend upon this primitive mindbodily logos. Language has the sinews of our bodies that had them first. *Dicto ergo sum.*

In short, then, the whole of our mutual world that we have caused to stand forth as oppugnant to ourselves from the background of the indeterminate other, in figures of our own devising, bespeaks on its every stratum that self-same logos that at once shapes and "hears" our beating hearts. *All* that is mediated by this logos is implicated with the actual world in which we live and move and have our being—as different as may be the form and "ontological" weight of these several expressions of worldly realities and as *various* as are their forms and weights from context to context. They are all, at given times, *fully accredited* participants in our world. In a given case, the Last Judgment is a more substantial reality of my (our) world than the tree outside my window.

"Then are you saying that the Last Judgment is as *real* as the tree?" "Well, the 'reality' of neither the Last Judgment nor the tree is context neutral. Each has its standing in the intricate system of meanings that constitute the world for us at a given moment, apart from which they *have* no standing; and their standing will be different according to which part of that system is, at the moment, the object of our focus and the subject of a particular interest. A tree—no matter how you slice it—is as different from the Last Judgment as a laser beam is from a quadratic equation. Nevertheless, a tree is no more intractably a part of our world than is the Last Judgment."

"Then are you saying that, in the appropriate context, what we used to call *myths,* with all its pejorative force, may be real vectors of the truth about the nature of things?" "As certainly as I would say, in the appropriate context, 'There is a tree outside my window' is such a vector."

6/2/92

The appearance of the phenomena that came to be called *aestheticism*—a term first applied (1895) to Tennyson's "The Lotus Eaters"—bore witness to the growing abandonment of "the mortal world" in favor of a poetic world answering alone to the forms of our affections, of the beauty of "music and pictures,"[s] of a place of unification and beatitude beyond the "Wasteland" of mere fragments of meaning left by "science" and "technology."

It was the despair of poesy; an open acknowledgment, at the level of theory about itself that was one of the major preoccupations of modernist poetry, of the triumph of the bifurcation of meaning into that which is shaped by the *real world* and that which only *shapes* our sensibility (the tropes, images, metaphors, figures, myths—in short, the inescapable "poetry" of ordinary speech—remained largely unnoticed), a fulfillment, at last, by the Industrial Revolution, of the Cartesian promises that submission to the disciplines of its method and, by implication, a subscription to its metaphysical dualism, would "enable us to arrive at knowledge highly useful in life . . . and thus render us the lords of nature."

In the twentieth century a so-called postmodernist critical theorist, J. Derrida, gave us his doctrine of *differance.* Demystified and deconstructed, this doctrine holds that in any given instance a word has at once to mean what it does in *this* context and also *not* mean all the things it does in all *other* contexts. Put in the paradoxical language that makes easy escape from philosophical accountability among his epigones, this is to say that a word means what it does not mean and does not mean what it means.

This is taken to be an at once quite shocking and exhilarating discovery, the very coup de grâce of meaning, even though the claim's actually quite benign import is comprehensible to a moderately intelligent ten-year-old

---

[s]Words used to characterize the Tennyson poem as an end in itself.

to whom even de Saussure and Heidegger are unknown and who is unlikely either to collapse into profound angst or fly into ecstasy at the news. If this is so, one needs to ask: Why?

The advocates of these views, believing that the only *conceivable* foundation for the meaning of a word would *have to be* its grounding in a static, eternally present logos—in this respect still hopelessly immured, for all its "radical" derring-do, by the imaginative universe that gave us *presence*—and, finding that there is no such ground, conclude that there can *be* no definite meaning to a word.

Innervated, in addition, by a romantic nihilism that is aestheticism turned inside out when all else is lost, it is inferred from the doctrine of *differance* that the meaning of all words is "always and everywhere" undecidable.

In theory, a sense that poesy has a bearing upon the real has long since vanished. Now language as such has slipped its moorings. This is the penultimate stage of our estrangement from our life. It remains only to take the ultimate step: the forswearing—necessarily *in silence,* of course—of the very language in which these putatively self-evident truths are propagated.

Poesy, without intending to, capitulated to the mind-body dualism that moves ubiquitously throughout this culture like an undertow—never so potent as when it does its work in silence. In ceding our bodies (and even our minds, to the extent that their natures are imagined to be reducible, as with Skinner and Freud, to objects amenable to scientific definition) to physics, chemistry, molecular biology, and such, it alienated itself from the living actuality of our mindbodies for which imagination, memory, and language are not contingent possibilities but ontological necessities.

Seizing upon what was left, it produced what might be called the *poetic body*—the word *body* being assimilated to the diction of poetry, in its way becoming as estranged from the mindbodily background of all meaning and meaning-discernment as 'body' *simpliciter.*

This loss of access to the only true authority and provenance of the imagination and language led quite easily to the linguistic nihilism of Derrida and de Man.

The inexorable working out of the logic of the mind-body dualism, itself the progeny of the hypertrophication of literacy values, has brought us to this dead end of *differance* and undecidability.

Imagination was sublined; and thus it was severed from its actual roots in our flesh, in our lively, sentient, oriented, motile mindbodies in the quotidian world, disaffiliated from the logos that informs and animates the provenance of all meaning and meaning discernment.

6/4/92

The intentional intervals between the no longer and the not yet that make up the texture of my life—whether these are, at a given moment, apprehended as extended or brief—are not abstract magnitudes of empty, atemporal visual space, but are richly filled with the concrete vectors within time of the actuality of my life. Whether it be that between my getting the tennis ball in focus and returning it to my opponent or the trajectory of my whole life from my earliest memories until this moment, the interval is proliferant with perceptions of all sorts, unfolding in time, that are, with varying degrees of clarity, recognized for what they are and, being *recognized,* named—or at least nameable; and whether named as such or not, they are fitted spontaneously into the warp and woof of the time of my sentient and oriented mind-body through the offices of the logos that enforms it through and through; in other words, through the agency of memory as the retrotension of the no longer and imagination as the pretension of the not yet.

I do not go about my quotidian chores giving, either silently to myself as an accompaniment to the unfolding of my perceptions in time or out loud to no one in particular, a narrative account of what is at that moment going on in my life. Yet if you were to interrupt and ask "What are you doing?" I should normally be able to give a narrative, either brief—one word—or extended; shallow—simply reading to you from my appointment book—or deep—such as are Augustine's *Confessions.* Within these narratives the present moment between a specific no longer and a specific not yet can be grasped.

The availability of such a narrative for explication is a *conditio sine qua non* of consciousness as such; it is the concrete embodiment of its intentionality. Imagination pretending the not yet and memory retrotending the no longer endow this tacit narrative with its liveliness and tone.

So much is true, after all, of even my English mastiff, Lex. He does not blunder about the world in a state of confusion but has, *because he demands it,* a coherent scenario of which his mistress and I and the home, of which he knows he is the stalwart guardian, are elements. In answering to his name in all manner of settings he shows he has a rich and continuous conception of who he is.

Even though the postmodernist theorist would appear to have to concede that *some* tacit narrative with *some* specific content is a necessity for life and consciousness, her own view would equally require her to question the authority of every *specific* narrative I might claim as *uniquely* expressing *my* self. For him or her it is necessarily the case that *every specific* narrative as the vector of a self is commutable; therefore, radically *contingent* with a force that could be fully felt only by one who supposes that the sole conceivable authorization of meaning disappeared when *presence,* conceived as a dead slice of visual space, became absent. There can therefore be no self (though I have seen no claim made by any of these writers that they are themselves not alive and conscious).

Nothing could serve better to show the utter abstraction from any *actual* world of the doctrines of these theories than the fact that for them the authority of the specific content of any narrative required to sustain life and consciousness must necessarily be, *even as I claim it as my own,* wholly undecidable. Thus, being asked while in the midst of writing *Speech and Phenomena:* "What are you doing," Derrida could only, in good faith (I do not know whether the meaning of *good faith,* applied by Derrida to his own utterance in the instant case, is meaningful because decidable; or if it is, how that can be), reply—in words the meaning of which could of course not *themselves* be undecidable—"I can't really say. It's all quite undecidable."

But of course there is no self as *static* presence; nor need there be, a fact overlooked by the postmodernist theorists, still bemused by their nostalgia for a lost *presence*—conceived as a dead slice of visual space.

Selfhood is an ethical category (in S. K.'s sense) because its existence is constituted—broken and renewed—in covenant. The specific narrative—tacit or express—within which, at a given moment, I experience myself as alive and conscious is the one to which I give my personal backing and within which I hold myself responsible.

But is this all we have? Yes. Is it good enough? No better ground for *personal* existence is conceivable.

6/8/92

Almost any ordinary sentence in the English language requires, has at hand and exhibits the same linguistic resources—tropes of various sorts: metaphors, figures, images, synechdoche, metonymy, amphiboly, irony; surplus of meaning, and etymological, that is to say, historically allusive, depth—and draws upon the same kind of human powers in the act of poesis as the first line of Shakespeare's *Henry V:* "O for a muse of fire that would ascend / The brightest heaven of invention . . ." no matter how threadbare these tropes will have become from repeated—and usually absentminded—use.

The fact that the one may be pedestrian, a commonplace, banal, lacking all freshness of language whereas the other is sublime because its language elevates us above the banausic world, induces in us new perceptions, and quickens the tone of our mindbodily life should not lead us to overlook the fundamental analogies. That we would think of the one as having the "literalness" of ordinary language whereas the other is "poetic," because of the power of its figures, should not blind us to the fact that imagination has an absolutely essential role in the making of each of them—thereby making clear that "ordinary language" and poetry are informed by a common logic and that what the dualism of Western philosophy led us to distinguish, on one hand, as "reason" and, on the other, pejoratively, as (mere) "imagination" are equal hosts and vectors of the real world.

Focusing upon the common *kinds* of linguistic resources of which they are fashioned and upon the exercise of the *kinds* of human powers required in their making, we can say that even ordinary language, clotted though it may be with cliché and moribund metaphors is made by the *same* human powers of the *same* stuff as that poetry which exalts us or fills us with pity and terror.

A word about "literal" and "figurative" is appropriate here.

A *literal* form of words has no other authority for being distinguished from a *figurative* one than that conferred upon it in our viva voce colloquy or, generally, in our speech community; *a stand is taken upon it as bedrock*—as the *O.E.D.,* in defining *metaphor* as "a figure of speech," does not take *a figure of speech* to be *metaphorical* (which it certainly is, being *itself* "a figure of speech") but instead *takes a stand* upon "figure of speech" as *literal:* as, that is, relative to this *definiens,* bedrock; else there will be no knot tied in the thread of language.

This of course will not satisfy the postcritical theorists, since for them the *only* thing that could privilege a form of discourse is its derivation from a transcendent eternally present logos that they, rightly, tell us is delusory—leaving them with nothing but the drab and false conclusion that "the meaning of words is always and everywhere undecidable."

One inference that might be—indeed has been—drawn from the disclosures of these formal analogies between "ordinary language" and "poetry" is that such *disanalogies* as may obtain between them are nevertheless not taken to offer adequate grounds for calling the latter *literature* and in so doing assigning a special value to it because it quickens our spirits and conveys to us a more substantial, because a richer, more complex reality.

Precisely this form of reductionism has been practiced by the more extreme postcritical theorists, as we have seen.

Despite these formal analogies, however, we rely quite skillfully upon the *disanalogies* between ordinary language and poetry, in appropriate contexts, to recognize and value the latter over the former.

But never mind that. I want only to establish that the privilege that a given linguistic vector may have as conveying what is "literally" the case is not the function of its supposed *independence* of certain formal linguistic resources upon which poetry is uniquely *dependent*—for as we have seen, no such independence can be claimed; nor are the human powers of imagination that issue in what we know to be poetry different *in kind* from those required to form a "literal" sentence in English.

To recognize this is to see again that the centuries-old bifurcation of reason and imagination is healed and to discover again that our lively, sentient, oriented, mobile mindbodies are the ambient ground from which all meaning and meaning discernment derive and in which they continually inhere.

6/10/92

Whether regarded at the moment of its intense focus through an electron microscope upon a molecule of unicellular life or through an optical telescope upon a quasar at the edge of space, whether it converges upon the events of the day just past or those of the siege of Troy, my self is the densest, the most concentered thing there is, the very paradigm of the concrete: the congealment of those things and events in the world that are of greatest value to me, of which the pretensions of imagination and the retrotensions of memory are the vectors and husbanders.

Imagination's pretensions toward ever-new coherences are directed from my mindbody upon its circumambient world of particular things and events, apart from which it would be powerless to call forth from the background of the indeterminate other new forms of meaning, new worldly realities.

Memory's retrotensions are directed from my mindbody upon the particular things and events of that world most valued by, because most necessary to, the integrity in time of my mindbody. When these particular things and events begin to fade from the fabric of the circumambient world memory goes slack. It is inextricably implicated with the usages and artifacts of our convivial mindbodily life in the midst of the cultural and natural world—even in the repertoire of our motor skills—for, conjoined with the pretensions of imagination, its retrotensions have caused a world to stand out against the background of the indeterminate other. Even so, the persistence of memory is vulnerable to any attrition in these cultural vectors of itself that it has conspired, with imagination, to form; nor is this fact of merely academic interest. In a culture in which "all that is solid melts into air," memory—which is to say, human being—is in mortal peril.

This self—my self, with all its worldly fellows—is of course always already imbedded in a tacit narrative structure provided by memory and imagination. Make this multilayered, overdetermined narrative explicit and critical and you have biography and history.

6/15/92

Observe a world-class long jumper standing at the take-off point at the end of the runway. If you abstract him from his context to focus more sharply upon the jumper himself—and this you do precisely by withholding the participation of your own lively mindbody from the rich texture of his setting in space and time, itself a feat of imagination—he may appear to be standing stock-still for many seconds.

Yet, if you begin to yield your own ductile, sentient mindbody to the particulars of the scene before you that jointly mean the whole that is the track and field meet, the isolate athlete (even to call him *this* is to have put him however thinly in a richer context) will begin to cease to appear to be standing stock-still and become instead a center of intensely concentrated potential kinesis.

Now allow yourself to dwell in the whole gestalt before you: the stadium, containing the spectators, but also the event as a whole; the other track and field events being run off; the public address announcer issuing the "first call for men's 100 meters"; the field of the women's 3000 meters, now in its last two laps, stretched out from the two leaders to the stragglers 100 meters back; the hurdlers on the infield stretching their hamstrings; the sprinters in the chute by turns bolting from their starting blocks for 10 yards down their lanes in rehearsal of their starts; and the focus of your attention, the long jumper, standing motionless at the head of the runway, in the midst of all. If, in other words, you give over your own mindbody as memory and imagination to the scene before you, you will dwell virtually in the long jumper's own largely unreflected summoning forth of memory and imagination from within *his* mindbody, they obedient to their own rhythms, as he is obedient to theirs. And this he does that there may be a world, with the concentration of energy that is his body at its center, into which he may launch himself as he begins his sprint down the runway toward the take-off bar and the sawdust pit beyond.

Even putting on your own pants requires, in small measure, memory and imagination understood in this way.

6/18/92

Thus our self-inflicted and near mortal wound is healed. In our practice—in *all* our noetic practice—there never could have been anything equivocal in memory's and imagination's grip upon the real world, from mathematical discoveries not yet made, to quasars at the edge of space, to the rage of Achilles before Troy, to the curvature of space-time, to the Holocaust's heart of darkness, to the circuitry of the central nervous system, to the angst in a Chopin ballade and the triumph of transcendence in Beethoven's Opus 132, to the reality of the "in-between" that opens when, face to face, you speak and I, in hearing, endorse you in your words—never could there have been anything equivocal in memory's and imagination's grip upon the real world, for they are in fact always the instruments of that grip.

"Imagination *is* redeemed from promiscuous fornication with her own images."

Appendix
For Whom Is the Real Existence of Values a Problem: Or, an Attempt to Show That the Obvious Is Plausible

A wasting disease has afflicted the human spirit, perhaps mortally, for now more than 300 years. We have, as Pascal saw at modernity's outset, simultaneously believed that we are gods and that we are nothing. This pitiless dialectic rends our souls from our bodies and suspends us in a lethal skepticism that at once flatters us and isolates us from our human reality: isolates us precisely by flattering us; flatters us precisely by isolating us.

Believing that the philosopher is a public man and therefore has a special vocation to the "space of appearance" in what Martin Heidegger called a "time of need," Maynard Adams, in two substantial and complementary books (as well as in countless essays), has with ingenuity and characteristic tenacity diagnosed and traced the etiology of what he does not hesitate to call "the derange-

---

Reprinted, from *Mind, Values and Culture: Essays In Honor of E. M. Adams,* ed. David Weissbord (Atascadero, Calif.: Ridgeview Publishing Co., 1989). Reprinted by permission of Ridgeview Publishing Co.

ment of the Western mind." This malady is the issue of the "gap between . . . our subjectivistic culture and the structure of reality."[a] We cannot "cope with reality and live successfully"[b] because our interpretation of our human powers is a false one. We no longer have access to the real. Against the ubiquitous and deep-going skepticism and subjectivism—in particular, value subjectivism—of modernity, Adams sets out to vindicate his claim that ". . . we can have a priori knowledge of the categorical structure of the world as it is in its semantic presence to us through knowledge of the constitutional principles of the mind or the logical grammar of language; and that it is reasonable to believe that the categorical structure of the world in its semantic presence to us is at least part of the structure of the world in its existential status, for . . . the mind is structured the way it is to make possible knowledge of the structure of the world."[c] One could not hope for a more lucid, measured or less tentative formulation of the view which more than any other modern subjectivism finds to be moot. For the sake of cultural therapy ("it is what philosophy, apart from its intrinsic intellectual value, is good for"[d]) Adams painstakingly adduces his arguments to support this claim. A formidable task indeed, for this is not a nicely defined dialectical Virginia Reel in which all the moves are set out in advance, but a counter-attack against a 300-year-old orthodoxy—an orthodoxy not of philosophers, not just of

[a]*Philosophy and the Modern Mind* (Chapel Hill: University of North Carolina Press, 1975), p. 54.

[b]Ibid.

[c]Ibid., p. 74.

[d]Ibid., p. 75.

philosophers, but of virtually all of this culture's vectors of meaning.

Adams, the philosopher as public man, has chosen to make himself answerable in behalf of his nonprofessional contemporaries and to prosecute his heterodox case before his most strict-constructionist professional judges. This course requires great energy and courage—to say nothing of wide conversancy with the literature of current philosophy—for such engagements hardly ever bring the satisfactions of a clear decision.

I shall instead embark upon an easier, even if less predictable course. Rather than taking modern subjectivism as a plausible philosophical problematic, I will, on the contrary, take my stand on radical "ontological" and "epistemological" ground[e] from which subjectivism in its modern Western guise cannot arise, even less therefore can it seem, on this ground, a possible point of view. From this vantage point, modern subjectivism in its doubts concerning the bearing of our thought and language upon reality in itself—particularly the bearing of our feats of evaluation upon values in themselves—will be recognized to be an absurdity. For of course to be alive is to be, throughout the whole hierarchy of our modes of being, ubiquitously, incessantly, unequivocally oriented toward values, concerning which there can be no *in principle* doubt; even our particular doubts in concrete situations are value-judgments that we had got it wrong or adjudications among conflicting values; even what we

---

[e]I have placed scare-quotes around these two words to indicate that, since my argument aspires to subvert the entire economy of concepts of the philosophic tradition, my use of these a fortiori varies radically from their use in that tradition.

call *facts* are the outcome of our sentient, motile and intentional mindbody's exigent pursuit of the most rudimental of all values: meaning, order, coherence and the real. This mindbodily radix in the world that each of us is is bedrock. More radical than, the antecessor and ground of all our truths of physics, biology, psychology; that out of which reflection's subject-object dichotomy arises, yet in which it cannot itself appear; that into which this dichotomy is resolved; it everywhere and relentlessly asserverates itself within the web of our ordinary ways of being and doing.

I do not hope that such an argument will issue in a more decisive outcome than that of Adams; nor that it will possess greater efficacy as cultural therapy. I do imagine that this line of inquiry, when juxtaposed to that of Adams, may put certain features, otherwise obscured, into sharp relief, enabling us to see that the obvious is indeed plausible: that values are real and ubiquitous and that no one in fact naturally doubts this.

The history of Roman Britain received an infusion when fliers noticed from the air certain slight elevations along the Scottish border with England not detectable from the ground. As was suspected they would, these proved to be Roman Walls, covered over by the centuries. We need to achieve an analogous detachment from the ground level of the philosophic tradition, if we are to see the obvious.

I

The distinction between a semantic object and an existential object, the distinction, that is to say, between what we think and say and something in itself about which we presume ourselves to be thinking and saying it, is on its face harmless and indeed can for certain particular purposes prove necessary, even though there is implicit in this very distinction a whole philosophy of language by which we could be heavily burdened, were it to go unrecognized. However, in the context of a certain repertoire of pictures[f] of our modes of being mindbodily in the world; visual, audial, proprioceptive, logical pictures that we both *have* and *are in the midst of* and that taken together form our theater of reflection, the distinction issues in the characteristic madness of modern subjectivism.

Now clearly this distinction and the whole problematic deriving from it has not arisen in the discovery that some *particular* assertion with its semantic object has on a *particular* occasion failed to bear upon an existential object answering to it. In such a case we recognize that we have got it wrong, and, remaining in this situation, we correct ourselves, go about setting it right. Only when our usual devices do not issue in that coherence demanded by our intentional mindbodies in their world; when, that is, our wonted ways of getting it right, judging we have gotten it right or, if wrong, going about setting it right has misfired, do we adopt a more reflective mode. Yet even here reflection is not obeying an *in principle* ecumenic skepticism. Its motive remains the confident search for a resolution of a *particular* incoherence which it has competently judged to exist. There is therefore not

[f]This notion is developed throughout my *Polanyian Meditations: In Search of a Post-Critical Logic* (Durham, N.C.: Duke University Press, 1985). See passim, but especially pp. 12, 293 n. 2, 14–15, 18–19, 58, 106, 150–51.

the slightest suggestion *in this actual case* taken in itself, that since we got it wrong we are obligated to make the relation between semantic objects and their presumptive existential correlates *problematic in principle;* and are therefore required to advance arguments to show that and how *in principle* we can ensure that our assertions can be made to bear upon the world. Our confidence is archaic that in our actual acts of assertion the semantic object bears upon an existential object—a formulation itself deeply implicated with the *in principle* skepticism of the philosophical tradition. By nature we trust ourselves in specific cases to recognize, soon or late, that we have got it wrong, if such should be the case, and to set it right—although, of course, when we are actually involved in what at this remove we call "a specific case," we usually do not think of it as *being* a specific case, that is, as being one of a class of cases, since our skills in this concrete setting are usually exhibited not in an obedience to explicit rules explicitly applied to cases, but in the tacit assent of our integral and oriented mindbodies to an emerging order, meaning, motif and coherence that the world offers us.

There is, quite simply, no logical space, no critical purchase here for an *in principle* ecumenic doubt. And this confidence necessarily has more authority over us than any arguments could that were advanced to support an *in principle* claim that, subject to specifiable logical and epistemic conditions, our semantic object will be brought to bear upon its presumptive existential object. For such authority as these arguments may be thought to have in themselves in fact descends from this archaic confidence.

How could we ever have been brought to think otherwise? I believe the answer lies in the regnancy in this culture for more than 300 years of an ecumenic *in principle* skepticism. Yet if what has just been said were true, whence this skepticism? If it has not been required by the discovery of our specific failures and their particular causes, by what then has it seemed required? What has accomplished our fateful seduction?

The skepticism of which I speak is nothing so explicit or "philosophical" as one that is embraced to afford methodological purchase, as Descartes, in his explicit justification, alleged his to be, although its permeation of the ethos in which we live and think owes much to this form of it, with its appeal to us that thus we can in reflection be as gods to ourselves and the world. Nor is it a presupposition that is more or less routinely made explicit in philosophic colloquy. Nor yet is it an unacknowledged presupposition susceptible of being disclosed by an argument ad hominem—though this moves in the right direction. This skepticism is yet more elusive because it is *radical* in relation to reflection: An obsessively recursive unmasking that continually displaces the authority for us of what is immediately real in favor of some hidden, often putatively ignominious, truth, a sour and clandestine nihilism that assures us that, even if we are nothing, at least we are not deceived; a distrust that afflicts us like a subclinical viral infection that saps the mindbodily energy with which we naturally bond with the world, or like a mild, chronic depression—which indeed it is—that seems pervasively to place a veil between ourselves and the deepest root of our well-being that is our mindbodily inherence in and affirmation of the world. It dissembles our real power while seducing us into a grandiose presumption of a power which is spurious. It obscures the fact that our *ultimate* relation therefore all of our *derived* relations to existence are fiduciary.

Beneath the derangement which is a function of "false philosophical assumptions about the constitutional principles and powers of the human mind"[g] there lie our hubris and infidelity.

It becomes necessary then for us to ask: If no ecumenic *in principle* skepticism is implied in our practice, even in the in course *ad hoc* revisions of that practice when we get it wrong, what device generates and sustains it, standing as it does in such a radical relation to reflection that it is hardly ever itself the subject of an act of reflection; how could we have come to believe that withholding assent has priority over granting it, not withstanding the fact that, as acts of our lively mindbodies seeking orientation within the matrix of the real, they are moved by precisely the same heuristic intentions, have identical weight as moments in our particular feats of knowing? I believe the answer will be found in a structure of the imagination that lies at reflection's back; and this I will call the *theater of reflection.*

When we interrupt the flow of our ordinary practical activity in the world in order to reflect,[h] that is to say,

---

[g]*Philosophy and the Modern Mind,* p. 54.

[h]There are serious conceptual risks, of course, in this very formulation. The philosophic tradition has, I believe, usually yielded to the seduction, implicit in the notion of 'reflection' as "an interruption of ordinary practical activity," of exaggerating the discontinuity between the *ratio* everywhere tacitly at work in our practice and that which has a more explicit standing in reflection. The drawing of any sharp dichotomy between the human powers exhibited in our practice and those in our theoretical reasoning is of a piece with that between extended things and thinking things and no less untenable. There can be no theory-neutral practice—except perhaps an attack of *grande*

"bend back upon" ourselves, we will find both ourselves and the objects of our curiosity presented in a certain fantasy-setting, upon some particular stage, in some singular theater both *in* which reflection is *given* and *upon* which reflection is *brought to bear.* My foregoing words, the issue of an act of reflection, *require* that I supply to myself such a fantasy-setting that the words themselves have entreated—even as my most ordinary and routine acts of speaking and understanding speech require it. The words "interrupt the flow of our ordinary practical activity in the world" simply cannot be understood without, because they are strictly meaningless apart from, the stage-setting which the very words themselves serve however tacitly to summon-forth in fantasy. Indeed, for me to understand written or spoken words, be they ever so routine, is precisely for my mindbody to perform the hermeneutical feat of providing the words I read or hear with the stage-settings that, in our form of life, the words themselves call forth. This theater is not itself the focus, but is rather the setting within which the focal events, namely acts of reflection and their objects, are depicted by us to ourselves as being situated.

Let me develop this notion of a theater of reflection. Suppose I ask myself: How should I describe the phenomena of reading? The words 'the phenomena of reading' are neutral, taken by themselves, as to whether I mean to describe reading silently or reading aloud to an audience. The same is true of my above words, "suppose I ask myself." When I suppose myself asking myself, what am I supposing? I am of course inviting myself and tacitly in-

---

mal—and our highest feats of reflective intellection are dependent upon tacit feats of rational appraisal, no less logically necessary and no less rational for being inexplicit.

viting you to undertake an inquiry. As I hear this question addressed to myself, do I imagine myself as in solitude or am I picturing myself saying the words, "suppose I ask myself," to several actually existent hearers—actually existent, that is, in my fantasy? Or alternatively, do I picture myself to myself as asking the question rhetorically—in such a way, that is to say, that I do not imagine my words, whether spoken or written, as being addressed to any particular actually existent person, but to mere anonymous solitary readers whose existence in my fantasy is even more equivocal and shadowy than are the *fantasy* "actually existent persons."

Now, it should be noted that my argument here is not concerned with the various theaters of reflection in which we might *conceivably* set the words, "How shall I describe the phenomena of reading in order then to reflect upon these phenomena?" nor is it concerned with empirical questions like, "Would most people in modern Western culture, when asked to reflect upon the phenomena of reading, set this question in a theater of solitude?" My argument is a transcendental one. My question therefore is: "How *must* we have depicted to ourselves our acts of granting and withholding assent such that we have come to conceive and continue to sustain our *in principle* ecumenic skepticism, even though this could not be implied in particular acts of doubting and affirming?" I have said that the words 'the phenomena of reading' and 'suppose I ask myself' are, as such, neutral as to whether the reading under examination is silent or aloud and whether I, to whom a question is to be addressed, am alone or in company. But of course they are *not* in fact neutral in this respect, for I have already claimed above that the words which were strictly neutral as to any fantasy stage-setting whatsoever would necessarily be meaningless. When actually uttering the words, I am *already* embarked from within my existing, intentional mindbody, oriented in space and time in each of many different senses, oriented in and by virtue of a history, oriented in and by virtue of a culture with its characteristic repertoire of paradigmatic images, metaphors, analogies, models, rhythms, figures, styles, affects, theaters of action, vectors of values and fantasies. If I am to consider the "phenomena of reading," I shall have to have before me a more or less determinate range of such phenomena and this is dependent upon a tacit choice having been made between, on one hand, the picture of reading as a silent, solitary act and, on the other, as a *viva voce* public occurrence. The phenomena which will appear before me in the theater of my reflection in the two cases will be very different. If the theater in which I depict myself to myself as reflecting is of the first sort, then my relation to the words I observe myself reading (in fantasy) is noncommital (merely "aesthetic" in Kierkegaard's sense). If on the other hand, the theater is of the second sort, my relation to my words is, by virtue of even just the *fantasy* presence of other persons, commital (ethical or, at least quasi-ethical in Kierkegaard's sense). In this theater there appears a phenomenon not present in the other; namely, the phenomenon "the possibility of an ethical bond between persons."

Now, here it is necessary to interrupt the flow of the argument in order to issue a warning. I assume that you are reading these words silently and alone. If this is the case, then I think it quite likely that as you consider their meaning and reflect upon the two fantasies which I have proposed, you will appropriate them *as in your own theater of solitude.* If so, then the probability is very great not only that nothing in your theater alludes to your full mindbodily being in the world (and an allusion is the most that there could be), but that, insofar as you have a picture of yourself as a reader while contemplating the meaning of my words and fantasies, it will likely be that of an essentially discarnate mind in a theater of solitude. If this should prove to be the case, you will be, if at all, only precariously in touch with the very existential mindbody who bears your proper name and is, *as you are just now reading these very words,* seated in your chair.

If all this should be the case—and this is the point that justifies my digression—then the *force* of the difference between the fantasy I have proposed of reading as a silent, solitary act and the one I have proposed of reading as a viva voce public occurrence could well be lost, since in order to recognize the difference between dwelling first in one fantasy world and then in the other, you must in some sense simultaneously retain real access to and tacit acknowledgment of your actually existent mindbody in the world.

So we are beset. We practice reflection, entrammeled by the imaginative devices of modernity and accomplish, in reflection—but not, alas, only there—the inconsolable loss of ourselves.

Now to continue. An actor memorizing his lines in solitude is one thing; his speaking them as the character he is before an audience is quite another. Between him and his audience—as indeed also between himself and the character he plays—there is a kind of implied quasi-contract, *even though* his words are not his own and will not be heard as if spoken uniquely to anyone in particular. His words in all their palpability take their place between him and his audience in a public space and time, thereby to have a quasi-ethical force. And, of course, even though the actor and the members of his audience do not engage one another as fully ethical beings—the proscenium ensures that his words *will* retain some of their merely aesthetic significance, for example, members of the audience will not intervene in the action on the stage—the difference between the fantasy world in the theater of solitude and this "interpersonal" even if fantasy world of self and other, impoverished though it be, is absolute. The theater of reflection that contains but a solitary and all but discarnate thinker is not less different from one in which, even if only in fantasy, a personal other can appear than are the cases of a private and a public reading; and they are analogously different. As we have observed, certain things—"an implied quasi-contract," for example—cannot be disclosed to reflection in the theater containing only a solitary thinker, for there, quite simply, it cannot appear.

Now, it is my supposition that the profoundest spiritual truth about most of us in modern Western Culture is that we experience ourselves as alone, not alone before God: just alone, *profoundly* alone—before the abyss whence God has absconded; that virtually all of the images through which we are mediated to ourselves converge to reenforce this experience and that therefore when we set ourselves a particular problem for reflection, we will, without reflecting upon it, cast that problem in a theater of solitude—in other words, for example, asking ourselves "How shall I describe the phenomena of reading?" we will take ourselves to mean reading silently in solitude. Were we at this critical moment to introduce even a mere *fantasy* other into this theater of reflection, it would move us from this ghostly place one modest but important step closer to the real world in which we find ourselves mindbodily rooted with our fellows in the firm rhythms and stout sinews of our actual life. But since we do not, we, in reflection, sever our bond with our actually existent mindbodies that are the omnipresent and inalienable matrix whence all our acts of indication flow, within which our feats of meaning-discernment are conceived and brought to term. Thus do we fatefully dissemble our radical and ingenuous semantic covenant with all that is richly over-against us as the world.

Now, let me animadvert upon certain features of the theater of solitude which, I have claimed, invests our imaginations and, as such an investment, has effected and nurtured our ecumenic *in principle* skepticism. Let us in particular ask more about its configurations and about how it accomplishes its lethal alienation of ourselves. And let it be remembered that, though I shall, in some detail, infer the logic of this theater that, in a sense, I shall have "invented" and appear to suggest that the matter is simple, though it surely is not, and that it has a broad range of logical efficacy over our imaginative life that it certainly could not, I shall pursue the analysis of this paradigm as if these demurrers were gratuitous. I do assume however that in my reflective life I always have at my back some such structure of fantasy and that it is not idiosyncratic but cultural.

As I reflect upon the silent and solitary act of reading, the first thing I notice is that it is *silent*. Not only is the reading *in* silence, the theater in which it occurs is withdrawn from the rich, sounding world by which I am, in reality, surrounded, which includes the omnipresent rhythm of my pulse—is it a sound, or is it something protomotoric, proprioceptive? I notice too that this theater is dominated by stasis: inert words statically juxtaposed upon a page in uniform rows with uniform spaces; all of the words on a single line of print having the same value to the beholding eye; the eyes that see taking in each line, taking in the whole page at a glance; the mind that understands what it reads doing so as if in an instant, the whole scene existing before me in a kind of eternity. I also notice that in this picture the mind's understanding of what is before it is detached and noncommital, analogous to the eyes' relation to the particulars which constitute the whole that they take in at a glance. There is no sense of a tension among the constituent words nor between the reader and the page from which he reads.

Now, it makes no sense whatsoever to speak of there being quasi-ethical bonds—indeed bonds of any kind—between the reader and his objects, as depicted in this theater of reflection; and it makes no sense to speak of there being bonds among the constituent particulars of what is before him in this depiction. This is of course because in this theater what we have is an all but discarnate mind opposed to an essentially static world of inert words. In the contrasting case in which we imagined an actor speaking his lines to an audience we observed that his uttered words took their place in a public world between his own body and those of the people before him; and we suggested that as this happens a quasi-ethical bond—a kind of contract—is tacitly negotiated between them. Just to *listen* to another person is to have entered, however thinly, however tentatively, into an ethical relation.

Even as a fantasy of a situation such as we might find ourselves in, even just as a theater of reflection, impoverished though it is compared to the rich reality of our actual way of being, the latter as a *picture* of ourselves in the world is superior to the theater of solitude.

Now while I do not of course claim that the theater of solitude is our only depiction of ourselves in reflection; or even that it is the preeminent one—although this may well be the case in the philosophic tradition—I do suspect that we are more immured in it than we have begun to imagine. This picture, which taken together with a coherent system of mutually implicative other images, metaphors and analogies, represents to us our relation to nature, to our own bodies, to the world of material objects, to time and history, to our acts of reflection, to our decisions, to our intellects, even to our own egos. We stand to ourselves and to the world as God is imagined to stand to the world he made out of nothing: essentially disembrangled, transcendent, autonomous. This is the picture in which the subject-object dichotomy is conceived; in which the discarnate ego is a certainty and everything else is problematic; in which semantic objects are secure and their existential correlates dubitable *in principle;* in which facts are inherent and values adventitious; in which all of our *de facto* bonds with the world have *de jure* been suspended. This is the picture, in short, that simultaneously flatters us and throws us into despair by isolating us from our actual incarnate human reality.

This theater of reflection of course, though not invented by Descartes, was brought to perfection by him. On his journey from the school at La Flêche to his solitary room during a German winter, he systematically severed his ties to the world established in his knowledge of ancient languages, fable, history, poesy, mathematics, morals, theology, philosophy and science (as then understood) to come at last—disarmed of everything save only the Latin and French languages, formidable links to history, to be sure, that Descartes seemed not to have noticed were still conveniently at hand—to surrender the existence of the external world and God. It hardly matters what happened next. What we have in this narrative is what became the paradigm for modernity of responsible reflection, the *conditio sine qua non* of veridical knowledge; and it would be impossible to exaggerate the thrall in which it holds us: an ecumenic *in principle* doubt that flatters us by tacitly assuring us that we are as gods to ourselves and to the world. The despair comes later.

This critique of the Cartesian faux pas is of course one that has been made a thousand times and it would be difficult to find voices which dissent from *explicit* formulations of it. For all of that, there remains at our backs almost universal *tacit* assent to this discredited Cartesian picture. Explicit philosophical efforts to challenge it—that almost no one is disposed to mount—would have roughly the same kind of efficacy as cultural therapy as would the statement "you want to kill your father so you can have your mother to yourself" would have as psychotherapy to a man suffering from profound but unrecognized Oedipal conflicts.

We saw how the picture of reading as a *viva voce* public event disclosed the possible existence of a quasi-ethical relation between the reader and those who hear him; that their presence to one another as mindbodies, jointly dwelling in the world which the spoken and heard words call into existence in their midst are bound to one another by the ligatures of their mutual place and time, of their sentience, of their motility—gross or fine-grained—of the web of their convivial affects. In short, it makes sense to say of the *dramatis personae* of even this fantasy theater that they are *persons,* bonded together in the world in a practically infinite number of ways, including the quasi-ethical way.

There are no such bonds in the theater of solitude. The solitary reader beholding the inert words before him can be primordially bonded to nothing. The conditions for such do not exist, since in this theater he is a discarnate mind, a discarnate eye in a kind of eternity before the page. Not depicted as present to the printed words as a sentient, oriented, intentional mindbody, the intentional bonds that necessarily exist between the words for *my* mindbody as *I* read cannot exist for him. Which is to say that the condition for the words being the particulars of a sentence and thus the bearers of meaning are absent. The logic of the theater of solitude rigorously followed to its end dissolves meaning. It is of course rescued from discard because our own mindbodies tacitly supply those features whose absence from this picture would render it absurd on its face. It is not just that this paradigmatic picture of ourselves in the world is one in which values become problematic; it is one in which, without those essential elements which it lacks being surreptitiously supplied, meaning, order, coherence and a world would be inconceivable. So we conspire in our bondage by tacitly denying our bondedness.

We all know quite well, on the contrary, that we are beings who exist in the midst of a plexus of bonds. The developing human infant is, in the womb, bonded to its mother, and this is a primordial—must we not say, *the* primordial—bond of our existence. The fact of our having been born into a world after nine months of uterine life is profoundly engraved upon, is ineradicable from the prehistory and still actively present in the history of our mindbodily being. No matter how far from this we may be abstracted into our later history, we still carry in our being as a living, present reality this archaic connection with the world, which nothing can supercede, no matter how strenuously we seek to deny it. Once born, we are bonded to our mother's breast, to our infant place, to our fathers, to our brothers and sisters, to the members of an extended family, to our human fellows on the face of the earth, to other animals and to all living things.

Now we need to look at the notion of bonding as such, for I shall be interpreting it in an unusual way and bending it to some unconventional uses. Since this is an attempt to extricate myself from the oppressive strictures of the theater of solitude in order to discover the form of what is at once our earliest, most archaic and only infrangible relation to the world, I shall adopt the first person, hoping thereby to avoid the conceptual pitfalls of a third person mode. For your part you would be well advised as you read to take up your own first person stance lest, translating *my* words into *your own third person,* you become a victim in turn.

Absolute bedrock for me is my own sentient, oriented, motile and intentional mindbody. It is through this that I have my first and continuing unmediated dynamic bond to all that constitutes my world. This mindbodily presence to the world is the temporal antecedent, logical ground and infrangible historical setting of all my mediated and reflected modes of being present to it. I am first and last—and all the time in between—an intentional mindbody in the world dialectically moving back and forth between the prereflective and reflection. This Being to which I have direct and absolutely indubitable access in my unappeasable sense of my own existence; this ground the nonexistence of which is inconceivable so long as I do not abscond from myself; this Reality that is an *absolute* by reference to which I am enabled to conceive the *relativity* of alternative worlds; this *arché* by relying upon which I am moved—first by my primitively oriented sentience and motility and then, in due course, by my ever more fully personal intellectual passions—to seek a reality commensurate with it; this radix which "shows itself" in the world of which it is the ground everywhere and relentlessly asseverates itself within the web of my ordinary ways of being. If the model for what it is for anything to be knowable is that it be a possible object opposing a subject, then this Being and the bond of my mindbody to it are not items of my knowledge, nor can they be. And yet for all of that, as I have said, it everywhere and relentlessly asseverates itself within my ordinary ways of being and doing. When reflection mediates the world of objects to me within the form of the subject-object opposition, thereby giving rise, *inter alia,* to common sense and to the sciences of biology, psychology and sociology, I can give a commentary upon those modes of my mindbodily appearance insofar as they are accessible to biological, psychological and sociological categories. But the continuing ubiquity of my unreflected mindbody as logical ground and as an abiding historical setting is the condition at once of the possibility of my grasping the meaning in themselves of biological, psychological and sociological categories and of my being able to bring them to bear upon those modes of its appearance accessible to them. No matter how estranged from this tonic and omnipresent archaic reality I may imagine myself to be—as, for example, in thinking myself to be contemplating "timeless" mathematical entities—I am always anchored in the world in this Being the non-existence of which is inconceivable.

Now, the foregoing being given, how are we to understand this fundamental fact about ourselves—that we exist in the midst of a plexus of bonds? Obviously we can give a biological account of the factors that promote the bonding of a fertile egg to the uterine wall, what promotes a healthy bond and what is the cause of a rupture in this when spontaneous abortion occurs. And in appropriate circumstances we can employ psychological and sociological categories to illuminate the relation between a mother and her child or the relation among the members of an extended family. And for the specific, limited purposes for which these are appropriate they are indispensable. It is the philosophical—more accurately, the bedrock ontological—claim, hardly ever explicitly tendered, almost always tacitly endorsed, that our human bonding to all to which we are bound is *radically* and *only* what biology or psychology or sociology say it is. The bond between me and my golden retriever, Wiz, is not the outcome of the felicitous utterance of performatives whose "happiness conditions" have been fulfilled. It is, on the contrary, the condition of their possibility. It is not the case that the biological account is radical, as I have said, because my earliest, most archaic and only infrangible relation to the world, is in the immediate presence to it of my intentional mindbody and because the necessary condition of my being able to make these sorts of commentary upon the modes of my mindbodily appearance that are accessible to them is the continuing dynamic presence of this logical ground and historical setting which my very being in the world is. If I use these derived categories to characterize the fundamental nature of my natal connection to the world to describe my existence in the midst of a plexus of bonds, then, on the one hand, *all* such bonds will be conceived to be merely *contingent,* inherently *frangible*—you might even say, dubitable *in principle*—and therefore it is not of the *essence of my being* to be infrangibly bonded to the world in this way; and, on the other hand, I cannot be conceived to be standing existentially upon a ground that is uniquely my own; rather I am but a plexus of contingent bonds. In short, I am not unlike the reader in the theater of solitude!

If, then, I am to take my bonding to the world to be inherent to my being as such, a necessary rather than a merely contingent relation, I shall have to recognize that my primordial bond to my mother who bore me, a bond that is efficacious even at this very moment as a mind-bodily memory from the earliest times of my existence, then I shall have to own that this bond is an ontologically radical one—rather than a mere biological one. Nature is indeed our mother and we are necessarily bonded to her.

Now that I no longer need to abide in the theater of reflection where the relation between my "body" and my "mind" is certain to prove problematic, where the "mind" is usually depicted as all but discarnate and the preeminent, if not the sole, seat of reason and the chief means by which I acquire knowledge; now, that is to say, that I am free to recognize that all of my activities are integral mindbodily ones, whether I am threading my way through a crowded room, interpreting my own behavior to a friend in psychoanalytic categories, or solving problems in calculus, I am emboldened to make the perhaps outlandish claim, that all my knowing is a bonding—ranging from the most archaic and immediate knowledge that I have as a developing infant in my mother's womb to the latest and most abstract feats of mathematical heuristics. How can I begin to make such a case?

Following suggestions implicit in what I have argued above, if we say that to understand bonding as a radical, as yet unreflected mindbodily relation, can we not say that it is also an indwelling. For me to be bonded is for me to indwell an "other," sometimes prereflectively, sometimes in reflection, from within my mindbody. In mindbodily indwelling an other, *any* other—the living cell I see through a microscope, the face of my beloved, a conceptual scheme, the grammar, syntax, semantics and etymology of my native language, the flight of migrating finches fluttering in the front yard like a shower of gold, the facets of a diamond, the morning excitement of my dogs when it is time to jog, the configurations of my mother's womb—I grasp its form, its logos, its meaning as it answers to the form, logos and meaning of my own integral and intentional mindbody. Thus to indwell an other is in the important sense to *know* it; to have had this knowledge is to be able to *remember* it, to bear it along and to reiterate it in myself—my intentional mindbody as my *pre*history and as the continuing lively ground of my ongoing *history.*

Of course this will entail that the most archaic sense I have of form, whole and meaning is grounded in the given, unreflected and prelingual integrity and natural gestalt of my tonic, sentient, oriented and motile mindbody within its interpersonal, convivial *mise en scène;* that I primitively and immediately know form, wholeness and meaning, for they are the radical existential modalities of my being in the world, long before I have words or concepts to embody this knowledge. Indeed, we must acknowledge it as the most proximate ground of our very power to generate words or concepts which we bring to bear upon that in the world, including ourselves, to which, also because of this archaic sense, we have discerned their appositeness. 'Form,' 'whole' and 'meaning,' as they appear in reflection, presuppose themselves prereflectively.

Now, what I have wished to show in all this is the fact that our ingenuous confidence that, soon or late, our "semantic objects" bear upon their "existential correlates" is ubiquitous and continually accompanied by because grounded in our own mindbodies in the world before reflection; and that this bond is antique, venerable and logically necessary—indeed the very touchstone of necessity. *This* is the *given,* that we, alas, can only awkwardly and equivocally *receive.*

And yet, even though *de facto* we exist amidst a plexus of bonds, *de jure* all the gnostic images of our being in the world can only see these as a *bondage,* a falling into a worldly prison from which we can alone be saved by the *gnosis* of our *in principle* ecumenic doubt. By contrast, only when we remember that nature is our mother can we embrace and affirm these bondings as the very substance of our incarnate existence. But of course in relation to nature, so we imagine, we are no longer children, but masters.

II

For all of our *in principle* scrupling over the question as to whether and, if so, under what conditions our semantic objects bear upon their presumed correlative existential objects, we have, in a less austere mood, acquiesced in the view that facts—however these are to be understood—have an intractability not possessed by values and that therefore they are inherent in the nature of things while values are adventitious.

It is necessary here to develop in detail the view that explicit distinctions between facts and values need not arise in the course of our unreflective practice—though of course they may; and that notwithstanding this, our skill at making tacit rational discriminations in the midst of our practice usually remains intact. It is sufficient for present purposes simply to remind ourselves that "facts" and "values" as we in general understand and evaluate these in modern Western culture are creatures of our reflected, second-order account of our doings and knowings. The conception of the sort of thing that a fact is and that a value is, and the standing they each have in an axiological and ontological hierarchy is implicit in the whole texture of this second-order account. It would not be true to say that, if our second-order account were altered, our practice would remain unchanged; nor could we say that our reflected account is not answerable to our actual doings. If both of these suggestions were true, we would have to believe that the practice of science and especially technology, science's culturally highly visible child, has had no influence upon the way we think about ourselves; and that the regnant second-order account had made no impact upon our practice. The relation between our on the whole unreflected practice and reflection is dialectical and is perhaps best investigated on a case by case basis. What is germane to the present discussion is this: The vexatious controversy in the modern Western philosophic tradition over the standing of facts and values has largely been a free-floating second-order colloquy having at most an only equivocal relation to our ordinary practical life, *even though what is implied in this life is of decisive import for this very colloquy.* Now, *in an important sense,* this second-order account of what facts *are,* what values *are* and how they stand in an ontological and axiological hierarchy is true only because we *take* it to be true. Through this account our culture at once gives articulation to some of its own deepest and most characteristic values and inspires the loyalty to these of its denizens. In one sense, as ourselves creatures of this culture, we are deeply implicated with these values and with this articulation—to pretend otherwise is an act of bad faith.

On the other hand, to recognize from the standpoint of other values and other articulations that are also native to this culture that the regnant view of facts and values is true for us only because we take it to be so is to claim for ourselves some measure of autonomy vis-à-vis modernity. There is available to us however a far more promising because a radical rather than a reactionary recourse in face of this discovery that has usually led directly to a relativism alternating between complacency and Angst: I mean the recourse we have to our sentient, motile, oriented and intentional mindbodies in their convivial setting as a ground, no matter how difficult of articulation, from which to challenge the culturally regnant view of the relation between facts and values and as the basis, too, for formulating an alternative to that view. The alternative epistemological and ontological ground onto which I have been trying to draw you is one upon which our feats of reflection and intellection—the exercise of our so-called higher powers—are seen to be rooted in and derivative of even our most primitive forms of sentience, motility and orientation: our "minds" are seen to be inextricably implicated with our "bodies"; our visible gestures and audible speech are seen to be connate with the meaning and integrity of our mindbodily existence; the motifs of our speaking are seen to be consanguine with those of our movement; our language is seen to be, even if singularly powerful, but *one* of the modes of our mindbodily expression, and to be analogous to and connatural with them all; its grammar, syntax, meaning, semantic and metaphorical intentionality is seen to be portended in the grammar, syntax, meaning and semantic intentionality of our mindbodies; and finally *language itself*—its grammar, syntax and especially its etymology—is seen to be pregnant in its own right with order, meaning, rationality and value and to retrotend these in its own prelingual mindbodily source and ground. In making these claims I have relied upon my own and have addressed an appeal to your radix in the world that everywhere and relentlessly asseverate themselves within the web of our ordinary ways of being.

Now, if the mindbodily tonicity of each of us and of all of us together is radical, a datum by which we are immediately, comprehensively and ubiquitously confronted within the most ordinary activities of being alive, that is, possessing tonus, in the world, then every expression of our being from simple orientation to speaking to—at least in this culture—the drawing of inferences within a logical calculus is informed by a *logos* directed toward order, meaning, rationality and value. If this is true for ourselves, can we imagine any creatures to whom we would willingly impute a human form of being of whom we would not believe this to be equally true? And, if *this* is the case, is it not plain that we are bonded to our fellow human beings "*extra*culturally," just as I am bonded to my golden retriever and he to me "extraculturally," so that we can then jointly educe a common "culture" composed of all of the rituals and routines that we jointly endorse, in which we understand one another and by means of which we can be faithful to one another. All human culture is thus rooted in this earliest, most archaic and most infrangible bond to the world in which all men and women deeply share and by means of which we have access to one another "cross-culturally."

This necessary ground is precisely the Being to which all men have an absolutely indubitable access in the convivial sense of their own existence to which they are infrangibly bonded, the non-existence of which is inconceivable; the Reality upon which they jointly rely through their omnipresent even if unreflected mind-bodies in the world to discover the meaning, order, coherence and reality that issue in the institutions of the culture and that everywhere and relentlessly asseverates itself in their ordinary being and doing. The modern mind, in the extremity of its alienation, finds it almost impossible to take seriously a truth so utterly mundane and exoteric.

Of course we all believe in, rely upon this primitive, "extracultural" bond. If we did not, we would never have launched our first anthropological field study; and if we did not continue to believe it, *even after embracing the doctrine of cultural relativism,* we would not make a return visit. How can it be that an assumption so deeply imbedded in our practice has no standing in our second-order accounts of our knowings and doings? Why, because in the theater of solitude these primitive bondings to ourselves and to one another have been eliminated.

The doctrine of "cultural relativism" is an invention of the European Enlightenment and there is a painful irony at its heart. It holds that since we do not have the standpoint of God, we cannot have access to any truth that is not merely relative to some particular time, place and culture—which is to say, according to this view, we cannot have access to truth. And yet, believing this, we systematically discredit ourselves as knowers by invoking a criterion of veridical knowledge that *necessarily* could have no bearing whatsoever for incarnate knowers, thereby failing to notice the means we have at hand for transcending *horizontally* our variously parochial standpoints even though we cannot transcend them *vertically.*

This doctrine and the deep pathos it begets is a creature of the Enlightenment's theater of solitude. For "cultural relativism" as a doctrine is not, after all, the perfectly ordinary commonsense recognition of the fact that people in different times and places do and say different things—even, indeed, at times find one another to be unintelligible. This is true of people even within what we think of as a single culture—let us say, Blacks and Whites in contemporary America. Rather, this doctrine is the outcome of a certain quite parochial way of *being struck by* and *articulating* these facts.

And how did we come to be so struck? We imagined, falsely, that a culture is composed exhaustively of elements that are either articulate or articulable; and therefore that we dwell in a culture through our "minds" rather than, as is the case, through our fully sentient, motile, self-orienting mindbodily beings.

This depiction of the situation encourages us to forget that even our access to the articulate and articulable elements in "our own culture" depends upon our full, convivial *mindbodily* presence in it; therefore it encourages us to overlook the fact that we can always rely upon a full range of the inarticulate modes of our being as the means of an *horizontal* access to the "culture of others."

The "problem of cultural relativism" is then the creature of the Enlightenment's theater of solitude whereby we are made to believe that only that relation to "another culture" such as a discarnate God might have is good enough, *even though we can have no such relation to "our own culture"*; just as the "problem of other minds" is the creature of our belief that only that knowledge of another mind such as a discarnate God might have is real knowledge, *even though we do not know our own minds in this way.* "Cultural relativism" is, in other words, an ideology, its pathos innervated by the pitiless dialectic between our self-aggrandizement and our nihilism.

With our new perspectives, finding ourselves and all our human fellows on solid common ground, we will feel the pathos of "the problem of cultural relativism" gradually drain away, and be enabled then to dwell with some serenity in the one and only culture that we have.

How then came we to this pass, to the belief that facts are hard and values soft? Specifically, seeing that, as I have said, distinctions between facts and values need not arise in the course of our unreflected practice—that, in short, the "hardness" of facts and the "softness" of values are not phenomena that force themselves upon us there—when did we, in the modern period, begin to make such a distinction in reflection, how did we come to make *this* one?

The concept of a fact is of course no more context-neutral than is any other. The word appears hundreds of times a day in the flux of changing contexts in ordinary discourse with a rich variety of meanings. Its etymological radical is of course the Latin *factum,* from *facere,* and means simply "a thing done." Among the entries for 'fact' in the *Oxford English Dictionary* are a thing done or performed; the making, doing or performing; something that has really occurred or is the case; truth, reality; the circumstances and incidents of a case as distinct from their legal bearing. It first appears in English in 1539.

In the sense in which there are "irreducible stubborn facts" for us there are none in the conceptual setting of Greek rationalism and in the residue of it in Medieval rationalism. What do I mean here by rationalism? I mean "aesthetic reason," reason that grasps finite configurations. I mean the belief that reality is finite, as a circle is finite, as the life-cycle of an organism is, as the course of nature through her seasons is—for this is what it means, in this view, to be real; and the belief that human reason—which in this view demands that its objects be of this sort—is adequate to it. In Greek rationalism the cosmos is taken not only to be finite, but to be eternal as well. Change is intelligible to reason because in this view it satisfies reason's demand. Change is intelligible because it is—as *we* should say—unreal, the endless repetition of a finite repertoire of possibilities which is what is *real* in the Greek view. Nothing *really* happens—as *we* would hold from our point of view—there are no novelties, no *real*—as we should say—contingencies.

Medieval rationalism is a rather more complicated business because the ax has already been laid at the root of the tree: The doctrine of creation and incarnation are about to shatter the Greek cosmos and aesthetic reason that is its complement. Among the fragments that remain will be—as we should say—*real* contingencies, *real* novelties, *real* change—in short, "irreducible stubborn facts," for the world which God has created by his irreducible, stubborn word is itself the very paradigm of the irreducible, stubborn fact.

In spite of all these harbingers, however, medieval science is closer to Greek science than it is to modern, which is to say, it is rationalistic in the sense defined. And this is to say that it is still teleological through and through.

But modern science does not arise simply because the concept of the irreducible, stubborn fact, in the sense defined, was discovered. Had this been the whole story, all that is likely to have resulted is that the *ad hoc* practical life where men arrive at practical solutions by relying upon their sentience and intelligence would be endorsed as the test of what makes sense and what does not, what is true and what not. But of course this is not all that was involved.

Before we arrive at the irreducible, stubborn fact that is for us problematically opposed to values, the power of mathematics has to be discovered and nature has in consequence to be bifurcated.

Galileo spoke for the whole of modernity when he declared that the book of nature is written in the language of mathematics. No idea has had such prosperity since he articulated it. There is no need to recapitulate the triumphs in our understanding of physical nature wrought by the succession of Galileo, Kepler, Newton and Einstein. They are before us for all to see.

Yet this was of course not to be without price. This mathematization of nature was to become and is today an at times cruel orthodoxy. In throwing out the rationalistic bath, the teleological baby was lost. Organismic concepts, sometimes by means of incredible dialectical exertions, were "reduced" to physical concepts, with the result as Whitehead remarked that this new physical science was left with a problem for thought it could not solve and that is mooted to this day: "Given configurations of matter with locomotion in space as assigned by physical laws, [how do we] account for living organisms."[i]

Behind this was the "bifurcation of nature," a division into primary and secondary qualities: nature that is extended in three dimensions and either at rest or in motion at a mensurable velocity and therefore consisting of primary—i.e., inherent qualities; and the nature which *we* have endowed with the adventitious, secondary qualities of colors, sounds and smells. It is here that the decisive distinction between "hard" facts and "soft" values is drawn, and notwithstanding the subtleties that have been introduced into physical theory, it is still this

[i]A. N. Whitehead, *Science and the Modern World* (New York: Macmillan Co., 1927), p. 80.

large idea of a nature which "is a dull affair, soundless, scentless, colourless"—and we can add, valueless—"merely the hurrying of material, endlessly, meaninglessly" that holds us in thrall. Nevertheless, sweeping, indispensable and triumphant though it is, as a model of knowledge, against the backdrop of the rich texture of the world of our ordinary experience, whose appearances have to be saved, and of our actual knowings which do not obey the conditions of this model, its legitimate authority can be seen to be parochial in the extreme. For here of course the issue is not that of the appropriateness to its objects of a certain mode of inquiry—about which there can be no dispute—but rather that of the felicity of this mode as a paradigm of all inquiry as such. And in a sense, all we would need do is just to look away for an instant and our enchantment would end. Yet the gravitational force of the philosophic tradition and of modern Western common sense, to the extent that it embodies that tradition, weighs too heavily upon us.

Now how does all this—mathematization and the bifurcation of nature—comport with the theater of solitude that, I have claimed, is definitive of our modern sensibility? Most happily.

As a language mathematics possesses no tenses, no demonstratives, no egocentric particulars and no pronouns in the first person nominative case (to mention only them). Mathematics cannot even make a reference to itself as a language within the terms of its own system of tokens. Far from these facts being counted as liabilities, they are rather taken as the marks of its absolute abstractness, its freedom as an internally coherent system from any actual world. However, mathematics is much more than just the language in which the book of nature is written by means of which we achieve our profoundest understanding and maximum control over her. It also exercises powerful sway over our imaginative life as the medium in which our paradigm of meaning is cast and as a schematic structural representation of the nature of things and of our relation to it, a picture that we both *have* and are *in the midst of*[j] and that, as I have suggested, does its work at reflection's back. On one hand, we have a language that is atemporal, ateleological, hence value-free and, on the other, a discarnate mathematicizer quite as atemporal and value-free as the language that he uses. Of course, it is most improbable that anyone has ever explicitly proposed such an image, therefore there would never have been the occasion for anyone to point out its strict untenability. And *this fact* is the source of its potency at reflection's back. It operates tacitly as part of a cluster of images that come to a focus in the theater of solitude.

In the bifurcation of nature, the compatability with the theater of solitude is even more obvious and striking: on the one hand, inane nature "hurrying endlessly, meaninglessly"; on the other, our thought, insofar as it can bear at all upon the real objects—"by our senses we know nothing of external objects beyond their figure [or situation], magnitude, and motion" (Descartes)—as spare and bleak as its objects, save only for the whole universe of supervenient secondary qualities.

I have said that all we need do to break the spell of this picture of ourselves in the world is to look away for an instant. Yet, how are we to do this? By, I suggest, occupying the radical epistemological and ontological ground that I have undertaken to articulate here, by acknowledging and claiming the ground on which we all

---

[j]See note f.

stand: our immediate unreflected sentient, oriented, motile and convivially intentional mindbodies in their world; from which arise all our pretensions to meaning, order, coherence and the real, that never ceases being retrotended by this meaning, order and reality. Since being alive is to be, throughout the whole heirarchy of our existential modes, oriented toward values concerning which there can be no *in principle* doubt; and since, as I have claimed, even what we call facts are the outcome of our exigent mindbodily pursuit of meaning, order, coherence and the real; the real existence of values cannot then be thought to be problematic *in principle.*

Before—both phylogenetically and ontogenetically before—there were any reflected facts and values, before there was a distinction between reason and will, between a cognitive relation and a (merely) intentional relation, there were our convivial mindbodies, the omnipresent, inalienable and logically necessary matrix of all meaning-discernment, intending the meaning, order, coherence and reality in the world which is complementary to the meaning, order, coherence and reality that we immediately grasp and dwell in as our own fundamental existential modalities; *after*—phylogenetically and ontogenetically after—facts and values, reason and will, cognitive relations and (merely) intentional ones have been reflected and distinguished our unreflected mindbodies *remain* the tacitly active ground and arché of all our feats of meaning-discernment which these feats themselves never cease to retrotend.

Finally, it will have to be said: Perhaps the whole colloquy on this topic in the philosophic tradition was from the outset wrongheaded; perhaps now, persisted in for so long, it has become a form of madness.

Index of Names

Analytic Index of Subjects